You're The Secret

MW00526494

Printed in the United States of America

FIRST EDITION

CONTENTS

Foreword by Joel Freeman PhD.

You're The Secret

Success Seed 11:
Develop The Mind and Heart of An Expert in Your   Profession

Success Seed 12:
Dedicate Yourself to Completing and Serving Others

Success Seed 13:
Be Totally Honest With Yourself and Others

Success Seed 14:
Determine Your Highest Priorities and Focus on Them Single-Mindedly

Success Seed 15:
Build a Reputation for Speed, Dependability and Punctuality

Success Seed 16:
Be poised and Ready to Move from Opportunity to Opportunity

Success Seed 17:
Practice Self Discipline in All You Do and Say

Success Seed 18:
Unleash Your Inner Man and His Unlimited Creative Potential

Success Seed 19:
Network With The Right People

Success Seed 20:
Take Excellent Care of Your Health

Success Seed 21:
Be Decisive, Precise and Action Oriented

Success Seed 22:
Failure Is Not Final Nor Is It Your Only Option

Success Seed 23:
Pass The Persistence Test; Persistence is Wisdom

You're The Secret

You're The Secret

FOREWORD by Joel Freeman, PhD.

When you read this book you will find that it's right on point providing wise, practical insight and advice that will help you in your life for the rest of your life.

Back in the spring of 2008 I received a phone call from a gentleman. He told me he'd run across one of my websites on the internet and discovered that I was the author of one my books entitled *"Return To Glory", (The Powerful Stirring of the Black Man)*. I told him that I was and he proceeded to tell me that he read the book a year or so before and how much he thoroughly enjoyed the book. He was surprised that he was able to call me so he immediately did. I can still remember the excitement in his voice and some of the things he shared with me. I knew then that here was a guy who had been given some special insight on life and the art of living effectively.

We agreed to stay in touch and I recall us saying to one another that we sensed a strong bond of friendship. We ended the call with us encouraging each other in our professional pursuits and promising that we would stay in touch and we've kept in touch with each other every sense. That one phone conversation nearly five years ago ignited a friendship that has continued up until the writing of this forward.

In my experience of being an author, lecturer and motivational speaker I have discovered that there can never be enough books written about encouraging and empowering people to live successfully in every walk of life.

The important and timely message found in the pages of this book should be read by everyone who is trying as hard as they can to make sense of life and living. Donald's message is simple to understand and straight forward in his approach in encouraging people toward a stronger commitment to self discovery.

In his book, *"You're The Secret" (The Seal Is Broken, The Secret Revealed)* Donald maintains that there has never been a secret and if there was one it would be this. And that is you are the secret because within you the reader is everything you need to be the successful person that you only now dream of. In this book you will discover that success and wealth creation is not something that you acquire or attain to but rather is your birthright and they and many others have been inside of your entire life even while you were in your mother's womb.

Wealth and Success along with other amazing attributes are lying dormant in every person right this very moment. They are your birthright if you will but it's up to you to develop the courage and will power to discover and apply them in your life. Every Spring Donald reminded me that this amazing thing happens all over the planet and that is in the most unlikely out of the way places and obvious places the earth will put on show of beautiful plants and flowers that will dazzle the senses. No one plants, waters or cultivates these flowers but they come up each year on time every time. But in all of their beauty and wonder those flowers and plants will bloom and by summers end most of them will be gone only to repeat the process again. But you are much more than that and significance of your contributions far greater.

This relevant book for our times because it serves to remind us once again that everything is possible if we just believe in ourselves and what has been entrusted to us as our birthright. In my opinion there can never be enough said when it comes to encouraging people towards achievable greatness. It is unique and important because Donald speaks to you from a level of understanding of having been one of those people who has struggled and overcame the same things and from forty years of listening and encouraging others to be empowered from within. Within you lay vast treasure troves, untold reserves and an abundance of untapped talent, potential, latent abilities just waiting for you to give them permission to help you succeed in your life journey.

As a writer of motivational books myself I am confident that *"You're The Secret"* by my friend and colleague Donald W. Burton will become a part of your permanent motivational

You're The Secret

library and will be a book you refer back to time and again for inspiration and insight.

I am certain that after having read Donald's book you will become more determined than ever to discover those success seeds within and learn to use tools and strategies to explore the uncharted potential within yourself.

This book is a must read for everyone you know who's wants to remove the mystery and mystique the smoke and the mirrors from success and wealth creation. Every young person needing to learn to chart their course early on in life and avoid the inevitable pitfalls that are sure to come will enjoy this book. Donald has stripped away the veil of uncertainty by challenging us to discover the secret in life that stares at us in the mirror each morning as we prepare for another day. The secret is us. We need look no further.

Wise and practical insight awaits you within the pages of "You're The Secret". Let this book encourage you and ignite your will to begin your journey of self discovery, self affirmation ad self motivation in a real, genuine and permanent way.

Joel A. Freeman, Ph.D.
 Professional Trainer & Coach
Author of "Return To Glory, The Powerful Stirring of the Black Man" and
"If No One Loves You, CREATE The Demand"
Baltimore, Maryland Area

PREFACE

"To Begin a Task is a Wonder to Unfold, To Complete a Task is Truly a Miracle to Behold"

Success is about acknowledging, choosing, activating and experiencing. First you acknowledge that the seeds to succeed are already in you. Second you must decide what you will choose to do with those seeds and thirdly by activating those seeds with correct information will determine your final outcome. And because of your diligence, you experience the amazing results your decisions which in turn will produce for you...wealth.

The most precious commodity on the planet comes and goes without fanfare, applause or farewell. It's there; then it's gone. You can't see it, hear it, taste it, touch it or smell it but you can sense that it's real and important. It's often measured by the rising and setting of the sun or by our elaborate and not so elaborate time pieces we call watches. Even they fall short of truly understanding the unsearchable immeasurable mysteries we call time. Time may be measured but never controlled. It can be acknowledged but never managed. Appreciated but never duplicated.

It never ceases to amaze me how quickly time passes without us realizing how many things have taken place all around and throughout the universe.

Everyone has the same amount of time during the course of a day. From the moment we wake until we go to bed, each one of us chooses how we utilize that day. We cannot manage time we can only manage our choices is what we will choose to do.

You're The Secret

Some say that life is like a roll-a-coaster. There's a surprise in every turn. Life is a mixture of succeeding and failing, standing and sitting, inhaling and exhaling, sleeping or waking, moving forward or standing still. Life in all of its grandeur is truly a wonder to behold and experience.

I've noticed that in life there is a truly astonishing phenomenon. It appears that people work very hard but experience very little consistent results from that all of that hard work. This amazes me and causes me to ask the question. How is it that in a society like ours where opportunities abound we have ninety-eight percent of the nation's wealth is controlled by only two percent of the population? The purpose of this book is to explore badly needed and valuable insights in order to learn how to utilize those opportunities for our personal benefit and the benefit of others.

The Dynamic Of Change Rests in the Power of Choice!

Change is usually referred to as a good thing. I choose to agree with that summation. This book is about change. Change for you, the reader and change for me, the writer. Change for you the reader because you will be challenged to move your life forward and fulfill your destiny. Change for me the writer because writing this manuscript has challenged me to face my failures and motivated me, to move my life forward with a clear understanding of where I'm going and a strategy of how to get there. The very fact that I'm writing this book gives testament to the fact that change is essential for success on any level of life.

I have no doubt that whether you read one sentence, one paragraph or this entire book; you will change for the better. Just like the snow and rain or even a teardrop that falls provides moisture to the earth, I am confident that from reading this book—whether you read everything from the title of the book or to the last paragraph or just the chapters you think you need— you will be challenged to changed. And change you will.

You're The Secret

I don't believe in secrets. What is unknown can be known and understood. I do believe that for whatever reasons, information that could have accelerated civilization along the human timeline in past generations was withheld from those who needed it the most; the masses. Think of the Dark Ages.

I also believe that there are those, in prior generations within the masses, who were shown this information but because of the foolishness in the hearts of men, they rejected the knowledge. Because of this, this information was not transferred to the next generation.

Only those who value knowledge and truth will know and understand what to do with it.

It is imperative to know where to find the right information at the right time. If you desire to achieve and have what you see in other people's lives, you must read about and seek out those with expertise in your field or the field you want to go into. Once you have found it, you must be willing and able to do something with this information in order to complete the cycle of success by transferring it to future generations.

These pages hold valuable insights that I will repeat from time to time so anyone can understand them and immediately put them to work in their lives. So note that I have, without hesitancy, intentionally repeated myself. The thoughts, strategies and action steps outlined in this book are offered in a simple, time tested, proven, and easy to follow format so that the information can be understood and these strategies can be quickly applied today in real time.

Starting now!

Good luck on your journey.

Your Choice. Your Life. Your Change.

DEDICATION

This book is dedicated to those who have yet to see themselves as the TRUE YOU. For those of you who have found yourself wandering in the desert of disillusionment and discontent, may you find solace, rest and refreshing in these pages.

Live Long, Live On, Live Strong,

Your Life, Your Choice.

Choose Well.

KNOWLEDGE

To have knowledge is a good thing.

To know how to use that knowledge is a better thing.

To know that knowledge must be

Used and used well is the best thing.

Knowledge is power

And power is that unexplainable force that causes

Everything in the universe to move forward.

Therefore it is in the knowing and doing of a thing

And the completion of that thing

Lays the true and lasting manifestations of dreams.

Live your dreams!

Live your dreams!

You're The Secret

INTRODUCTION
The Life Is In the Seed

In the spring of 1970 I was sitting in my freshman class on the third floor of the Old Main Building on the McCurry College in Abilene, Texas campus when it began to snow. Imagine snow in West Texas in the spring. As the professor—who was the first to observe this wonder—finally got our attention and turned our focus back to our studies, we were instructed to turn to the introduction page of the Religion 101 text book. I can still see the book in my hand, feel the smooth texture of the pages between my finger tips, smell the paper in my nostrils and hear the turn of each page like it was yesterday. In the author's first paragraph there was a question.

The question read: 'If you take an apple seed and chop it into small pieces that are no longer recognizable then grind it into powder and blow it away, what do you have left?'

The question was intentionally left open. I didn't know what to think then. Over the years, however, I have drawn the conclusion that what remains of the seed is its true reality, its essence, its true identity and not just its manifestation called a seed. The things we see were made from things we don't see so the apple seed returned to its original state. The seed never disappeared; its appearance merely changed. The energy and life of that seed continued to exist.

At that time, my 18 year old freshman brain couldn't wrap itself around such a concept. The question challenged me to think in a way I never knew existed. The author accomplished what he set out to do; challenge a young man, who thought he knew everything, to realize that his journey and quest for truth had just begun.

Success is predictable, quantifiable, calculable and sustainable. If you want to be a successful person you must predict and strategically plan for it.

Success. It's already in you. It's in your DNA, your Genetic code; you were geared and designed for it. It's what you do with it and the way you nurture it that will determine its outcome in your life. Success is not a matter of guess work, luck, accident, or even being in the right place at the right time. Success is doing things intentionally and on purpose. It is the willful mental action of combining your dreams, thoughts, beliefs, emotions, feelings, desires, and core attributes into one harmonious whole. It is as predictable as the sun rising and setting or the perpetual crashing of the waves against the shore.

By practicing the principles outlined in this book, you will move your life to the front of the line. You will have an amazing advantage over people who have not discovered or care to discover these wonderful truths. The very fact that you are reading this book tells me that you're the kind of person who has a great hunger for success. You are a Truth Seeker. I have no doubt that you will put these principles into action and immediately begin practicing these techniques and strategies. If you do this, you will have an advantage that will give you the winning edge in your career choices and life—for the rest of your life.

When you set your mind to do the things that all successful people do and commit to being consistent and persistent, nothing in this world will be impossible for you to accomplish. You are the architect of your own destiny. You're the master of your own fate. You are behind the steering wheel of your own life. The only limitations to what you can do, have or become are the limitations you place on yourself by your own way of thinking.

You're The Secret

You are as good as or better than anyone you will ever meet. You are an outstanding human being. You have M.A.T.T. ™ on your side: MIND, ABILITY, TALENT, and TIME. You have an amazing MIND to create and imagine with. You have untold awesome ABILITIES to be productive, unsearchable TALENTS to explore unlimited possibilities with, and the same amount of TIME that everyone else has to accomplish your destiny with. M.A.T.T. is at your disposal 24 hours of every day. If you are to realize your hopes, dreams and aspirations, you will need to learn how to tap into your unlimited wellspring of M.A.T.T.

Your greatest responsibility is to dream big dreams. Decide exactly what you want, make a plan to achieve it, learn the principles taught in this book, take action every single day in the direction of your goals, and resolve to never, never, never give up, give in or give out on yourself or your dreams. You will discover a strong sense of confidence takes up residence deep inside of you when you take these steps. You become unstoppable and your success becomes inevitable. The entire universe will come to your aide to make sure that you accomplish what you have set your heart to do. Your success begins in your mindset.

I'm not introducing a new revelation on the subject of success and wealth. I think it's important for you to know that. These principles have been spoken for thousands of years and will continue to be spoken for thousands of years to come. I have introduced incites within these pages to reacquaint you with some truths you already know and make others aware of truths to consider for the first time and serve you well on your journey. Remember the old saying, 'When the student is ready, the teacher is there'.

Success Is A Choice. It's Your Choice. Enjoy Your Journey.

SUCCESS SEED 1

The Law of Thought

It is the mind, therefore, which overcomes environment and every other obstacle in the path of men. When the creative power of thought is fully understood,

Its effect will be seen to be marvelous.

-Charles Hanaal

It all begins with you and the way you think about everything. Success begins in your mind, thoughts and heart. All that you think and feel, say and do is connected. What you choose to think about will have a direct impact on you and everyone around you.

One of the things I've discovered about successful people is that they think, act and feel differently about everything and everyone around them. They don't waste valuable mind time thinking about things they know will undermined, sabotage, delay or abort their dreams and goals. When they encounter good or bad situations, they have trained and conditioned themselves to respond in the most appropriate way possible for that situation. They have learned to give themselves a specific amount of time to solve a problem, and make the right decision while they are moving forward. They understand that life and the universe is always moving forward and they've learned how to move and flow with it. They never stop moving forward.

You're The Secret

In the course of day how have you disciplined, trained and conditioned yourself in dealing with life's challenges as well as its opportunities? As you know, the vast majority of our frustrations come directly from other people and how we choose to respond to what they say and do.

Unfortunately, we can't deliver ourselves from others and they can't deliver themselves from us because we are necessary to each other on our road to success. What we can do, however, is determine beforehand that we will not allow the situations that come our way to clutter our thoughts and thereby render us paralyzed in knowing what to do next. Instead, we can use the power of our thoughts to train and condition ourselves beforehand to decide how we will respond to these people and situations whether they are obstacles or opportunities. The choice always remains with us.

What do you find yourself thinking a great deal? What's on your mind most of the time? Whatever you spend your time thinking about on a regular basis, is what you are training yourself to become. In other words, you become what you think and speak about. Most people spend a lot of time rehashing what people have said to them, done to them or the way they've been treated or still being treated. People spend a tremendous amount of time being overwhelmed by and speaking of things they have absolutely no control over...or shall I say... they perceive they have no control over. And, all too often they end up being overwhelmed by their thoughts and the things going on around them.

This kind of mental conditioning goes back years and each time something similar or the same thing happens, the mind immediately retrieves the worn out recordings found in the archives of past hurt, disappointments and mistrust and dwells on it once again only to find themselves trapped in time.

Through the techniques in this book you will discover:

1.   How to activate the archives of past successes, triumphs and untold victories to dwell upon that will catapult you forward into even greater successes.

2.   How to overcome the memories and present circumstances that undermine and threaten your future.

3.   How to lay hold of the memories you can build upon that will insure greater successes in both now and in the future.

Your mind is the new and final frontier, the untamed wilderness of your soul, and the untapped gold, platinum, silver and oil reserves of your amazing unlimited potential. Your thoughts are the tools and resources you need to begin mining these vast hidden reserves. It's time to get started.

Have you ever wondered how some people seem to attract success, wealth, power, fame, achievement and overcome tremendous difficulty with very little intentional effort? What about those who never seem to get out of the starting blocks and fail altogether in reaching their goals? These people relegate themselves to blaming of others; especially successful people, themselves or anyone else for that matter. They take no responsibility for what they have created and are creating.

What is the reason for this dynamic? Why do some people accomplish their goals easily and others have all kinds of

You're The Secret

difficulty over long periods of time? And still others _never_ get off the bench and get in the game. WOW! That's amazing to me.

These dynamics make the so-called less fortunate feel like life isn't fair. It causes them to ask, 'why do some people get all of the breaks or have all of the luck'.

But at the same time, society is filled with stories of other less fortunate's being very successful in life. Why is it that some less fortunate's can succeed and become extremely wealthy where others fail terribly even if they are from the same family?

What is the reason? It's not education because there have been people throughout history, with little or no formal education, that became wealthy. Neither could the cause be racial, ethnic or geographical because then you'd only have people from successful affluent families and communities around the world who would become wealthy.

The truth of the matter is that out of all the millionaires in America right now more than 86 percent are self-made and the number is growing by 15 to 20 percent each year. These successful people often came from very humble beginnings and broke families. In light of this, ask yourself what is keeping you from attaining to the level of success that you only think and dream about.

It's time you discover what these self made millionaires discovered. Learn these success seeds and join the growing number of Americans who are experiencing rapid wealth in our society every day.

You're The Secret

Together let's discover what it takes to join the growing ranks of the successful. Let's embark on a journey of self-discovery and

inner insight that will keep us from squandering our lives away in the desolate desert of debt, discontent and despair.

Successful people have discovered something very important and fundamental. They have realized that their mind is the engine that moves the train of dreams forward. It's the processor that organizes dreams and thoughts into bite size pieces called goal accomplishing strategies. Their mind's is the power plant of imagination that turns the wheels of the world. It provides untold opportunities and wealth for the weary traveler who would dare turn aside and drink the waters of wisdom from the oasis of truth.

This *is* the difference. This *is* the way successful people succeed. They train themselves to use their minds and focus on what they want to achieve. They continually practice the development of the creative forces of their mind and become relentless in the pursuit of excellent thought. They know that this and this alone is what constitutes the difference among men.

As a man thinks in his heart, so is he. The way you choose to think, perceive and respond will overcome environment and every obstacle in your path. Some choose to see the glass half empty while others choose to see it half full. It all depends on your perception.

You will be truly amazed when you understand and embrace the creative power of righteous thoughts followed by righteous actions. You will discover in this book that just as the laws that govern our physical world are fixed and absolute, the laws that govern the mental and spiritual world are fixed and infallible as

You're The Secret

well. And, we can rely on them to help us to understand and make sense of our surroundings.

If you are to embrace your desired results, then it is imperative that you know these unchangeable laws and work in cooperation with them. You must set your heart to understand and your mind to know what has been made available to you. By properly aligning yourself with these laws, you will produce the desired results with precision and predictability.

First, you must acknowledge that you are weak because you have relied upon and been influenced by false information from your five senses and wrong outside sources. Next, you must realize that power comes from having and applying the correct knowledge from within yourself. Then you can, with courage and boldness, throw yourself upon your own righteous thoughts. You will instantly become self correcting and stand erect. Assuming a dominant attitude, you will become a worker of miracles that changes the course of your life.

If you fail to fully explore and take advantage of the untapped seeds of greatness that lie dormant inside of you, you will soon be left far behind. Don't be the one who refuses to recognize and accept past generational knowledge written down and left for you to learn and apply. Find it. Embrace it. Learn it and then apply it.

Envying and criticizing the man who has attained a certain standard of living, financial prosperity and personal achievement wastes valuable and precious mind time. Instead, concentrate on how they accomplished their goals by diligent effort and a strong work ethic. Study what they are doing to sustain their wealth. Start filling your mind with the right kind of knowledge and information. Your journey begins with your mind, thoughts and your heart. Your Choice. Your Life. Your Change.

Begin the journey.

SUCCESS SEED 2

Get the Right
Information the First Time

The information you need to determine where and when is different from the information you need to determine why.

-Steven Speer

Information is plentiful. People are always ready to share information whether it's good or bad, right or wrong, complete or incomplete. They will convince you that they're information is the best. Have you ever been lost in an unfamiliar city and tried to get directions? Were you given incomplete information or worst yet, the wrong information? You would have been better off if they would have just told you they didn't know, right?

24 hours of the day 7 days a week and 365 days of the year for the rest of your life you are doing one of the following; downloading, processing and uploading good or bad, right or wrong, complete or incomplete information. Yes, even while you're asleep, your mind is active in your dream state giving you still more good or bad information.

Everything you see, hear, taste, touch and smell is influencing the way you think, what you do, how you feel and how you choose to conduct yourself. Your brain, your mind and your body are processing that information in real time and deciding what to do with each experience. After the information has been downloaded and processed, it is then uploaded back into your surroundings and the universe in the form of thoughts, conversations, body language, feelings, emotions and perceptions.

All of this happens in a fraction of a section, days, weeks, months and sometimes years. It all depends on the information you receive. Sometimes, it will take years to process the information before you can draw a conclusion about it. Just like there is a time cycle between planting a seed and reaping the harvest, the initial information you receive sometimes requires additional information before it comes to fruition.

Successful people have learned to make sure the information they use is the most accurate information available to them. They know how vital having the right information is; so, they surround themselves with people they trust to give them correct information.

Never be intimidated by people who know more than you even if they may appear to be arrogant or boastful at times. Remember you're there for sound reliable information

All too often we let personality differences stop us from obtaining the accurate information we need. You can receive good information from a donkey if you're willing to listen.

Make a habit of finding the right informational sources the first time. Why is this so important? It increases your chances of making sound choices and decisions. Your future success as well as that of others is at stake. People who have a reputation of making good decisions are always in very high demand and extremely well paid for their expertise.

If you intend to join the ranks of successful people, you must understand that knowledge is power and power is focused mental energy. Energy you can posses by training yourself through practice and use of these simple principles.

You're The Secret

You need the right information for the following three reasons:

1.   To make informed decisions about your next step in your success journey. You need to develop the skill of making sure your information is correct. For instance, you don't get financial advice from an individual who has less money than you. Neither do you get advice about your heart from your auto mechanic.

2.   To strategically plan your navigational route through the storms of business decisions that must be made on a daily basis. Having the right information allows you to accelerate the success process and shorten the timeline required for you to achieve your goals and objectives. The right principles you use to will help you to become financially secure and will propel you to millionaire or billionaire status if that's what you desire. You must keep learning and applying the same principles.

3.   To enable you to create a skill set of precision in your decision making abilities. Success requires split second timing. This type of skill can only be acquired by practice using your acquired correct, solid, dependable information and personal experiences. Never be afraid to fail or succeed. Keep moving your life forward.

You will need courage and strength of hear if you intend to be successful. Fearful people surround themselves with people who know less than they do. Successful people surround themselves with people who know more than they do.

If you can't get an audience with knowledgeable people, educate yourself by reading about successful people, listening to audio CDs, watching training DVDs and attending seminars dealing with your chosen profession and reading success magazines.

Never be afraid to say that you don't know. Always be ready to say you're interested in knowing more.

You're The Secret

- ·   Successful people are very good listeners.
- ·   Broke and broken people aren't.
- ·   Successful people will listen and learn and increase in wisdom and understanding.
- ·   Broke and broken people will maintain their position to their own demise and not even realize what they've done to undermine their personal success.

SUCCESS SEED 3

Dream Big, Think Big, Believe Big

I Like Thinking Big. If You're Going to Be Thinking Anything

You Might As Well Think Big.
                                        -Donald Trump

Your mind was created to dream big. Getting the right information makes those dreams come true. THE THIRD SEED of successful people is simple: They **Dream Big, Think Big and Believe Big!** They never stop! They never stop dreaming. Never stop thinking. Never stop believing. *NEVER!* They are driven to dream and their dreams are the driving force behind greater levels of personal achievement.

Stopping is not an option for successful people. My mother is 83 years better and she still dreams, thinks, and believes about the things she wants to do with her life.

Give yourself permission to dream. Think about your dreams, believe in your dreams and do something to move toward your dreams being fulfilled every day. Giving yourself permission to imagine and fantasize about the kind of life you would like to live and the kind of person you would like to be, is the most powerful thing you can do. Fix your thoughts on the amount of money you would like to draw to yourself. See it on your bank statements at the end of each month. Imagine pulling it out of your wallet and paying cash for that new TV or car.

You're The Secret

Have you given up on your dream? Most people have. Take your dreams out, dust them off and allow yourself to dream again. You say that's for others but not for you? Here's the kicker. The same way you have been talking yourself out of your birthright of success, is the same way to talk yourself into it. Try it. Start today. What do you have to lose?

Dreams don't come true without a dreamer. Everything on this planet had a starting point. Somebody dreamt it and decided to make it happen. For example, people dream of having a family to love and take care of so, they keep moving toward that goal until they have a family. Henry Ford dreamed of a card that the average American could buy and he made that dream come true. All I'm saying is that same dream dynamic applies to every aspect of your life. Start dreaming the rest of your success story and cause it to come into reality.

Remember, no matter what their walk of life, all great men and women started with a dream. They all had a jumping off point.

In order for your dreams to become reality you have to change the way you think. You must become mind image conscientious. In other words, you have to begin using your mind for what it was intended for. IMAGINING! I like to say "imaging your future" Your mind is geared like a high speed racing engine. In the right car with the right driver winning is all there's left to do. All you've got to do is get in and drive your imagination straight to the finish line.

Imagine that you have no limitations on what you can be, have or do with your life and for other people. Imagine that you have all the time, money, education, experience, friends, contacts and resources you need to achieve what you want in life. All of these things can be acquired over time.

Remember, you're drawing something or someone to yourself every day. It either affects your life positively or negatively. You might as well start bringing the things you really want into your life by changing what you choose to think about. So, take control

You're The Secret

over what comes your way by taking control over what kinds of thoughts you think about.

If your potential were completely unlimited, what kind of a life would you create for yourself, your family, your friends, and the world you live in? It *is* your choice.

If you're like 90% of the people I've asked that question, your answer is 'I've never thought about it'. That's ok but now it's time to do something about it.

Much of the human population is satisfied with where they are because they've convinced themselves they have achieved it by simply thinking about it.

Now is a great time to stop just merely thinking about it and move forward into the realm of dreaming about it, believing it and doing it. You will discover that your only limitation is your own imagination and that IMAGE-ENGINE-NATION called your imagination belongs to you. You are the success story. Write your never ending story.

There are no costs, taxes or penalties or penalties on the use of your incredible IMAGE-ENGINE-NATION *called your imagination.*

You should make it an ongoing practice each day to develop the powerful skill of *"seeing your ending from your beginning"*. This principle is alive and well in you already. You may not realize it but you use it every day. It's called planning. It's the ability to decide what you're going to do and then begin to develop a step by step strategy to accomplish it. Whether it' saving money to buy a house, car, boat or going on a summer vacation. You see yourself their before you arrive. You calculate what it will cost you in mind, ability; talent and time to make it

You're The Secret

happen then you make plans to make it happen. Start to use the tools you already have at your disposal in

Successful people think and practice this way of living every day. For them it has become like breathing. They no longer have to think about it. They have become it. They have trained themselves to do it on another level of productivity and production. That's why they are successful. Unfortunately, most people exercise this astounding ability in survival mode only and never pay attention to this wonderful gift at their finger tips.

Look down the road five years into your future. What does your life look like? What are you doing? Where are you living? How much money are you attracting to yourself? Who are your friends and associates? What are people saying about the kind of person you are? What would you like them to say about you? By making these choices today you are able to secure those harvests tomorrow.

Every farmer that has planted a crop understands this principle or he would never farm. He knows that victory loves preparation.

Without a vision the people perish or come to zero and accomplish very little in life. Create a vision for yourself for the long-term future, one that includes your great-great grand children and beyond.

In my opinion your vision should include at least 200 years out or more. Yes, that's right. It's called a legacy. People have been doing it for generations. History is complete with stories of people who did this. People like Andrew Carnegie, Henry Ford, Bill Gates and Oprah Winfrey just to mention a few. These people have chosen to leave vast fortunes of wealth to improve the lives of not only their families but the international community as well.

All you need to do is to read world history to discover that men and women have been doing this for thousands of years. The founding fathers of the United States of America understood

You're The Secret

this principle when they framed the constitution. We are the recipients of their visions and dreams and so will be generations in the future. We are the direct beneficiaries of their dreams, thoughts and beliefs that a better country was possible.

They did it; so can you. Your vision should include what I call "The Five Corners of True Wealth.´

1. Spiritual and Emotional Wealth
2. Educational Wealth (both formal and informal education)
3. Physical Wealth
4. Relational Wealth (you need good friends)
5. Financial Wealth

These five corners will provide you with the ability to not only obtain but sustain wealth for you and your family for generations to come.

When you have clear and precise mental picture of where you are going in life, you become more positive, motivated, and determined to make your dreams a reality. Dreams are your reality waiting to be birthed into everyday existence for others to enjoy. When you dream, an amazing level of creativity and ingenuity is awakened inside of you. You will have ideas upon ideas in how to effectively serve yourself and others in the pursuit and accomplishment of what you have set out to do.

Your actions must always move in the direction of your core, the seat of who you are; the real and true you. Your hopes, dreams, thoughts, mental/visual images and visions emanate from your core. You release a powerful dynamic within yourself when you allow yourself to dream big, think big and believe big. It does something you internally. You will never again settle for being less than who you truly are and the person you can be. It elevates your self-awareness and creates sense of self like and true self respect. It supercharges you from the inside like nothing else. It improves your self-perception. It raises your level of confidence and joy. It makes you want to be a better you.

You're The Secret

It just feels right. Dreams are exhilarating, empowering, powerful and eternal. Dreams are what the universe is made of. Ask yourself: **What one thing would I dare to dream if I knew I could not fail?**

Think of one amazing goal you would be bold enough to dream—dare to dream—if you absolutely knew you could not fail. What would that goal look like, sound like, smell like, taste like and feel like? If your success was totally guaranteed short-term, long-term, great or small, what would your perfect life look like?

Now, write it down and start imagining that you have achieved and are doing working toward this great goal already and you can see it coming towards you as well. As you draw towards it, it will draw towards you. *Visualize, visualize, visualize until you can see it already accomplished in your mind and believe it in your heart because when you see it in your mind, it is done.*

Okay, you see it clearly. Now, what do you need to do to begin working toward the vision you see in your mind's eye.

Now, how do you move the vision from your mind to the real world? Here's how you do it. Ask these questions:

1.   What are the steps you took in your thought process to accomplish your goals   that you need to put it into action in the real world?
2.   What psychological strategies did you develop to accomplish your objectives?
3.   What changes did you make in your life; physical, mental, financial and spiritual?
4.   What did you have to start or stop doing?
5.   Who did you see yourself working with? Who was no longer be working with you?

Dreaming Big Thinking Big and Believing Big is vital for achieving your goals for financial independence and beyond.

You're The Secret

The primary reason that people never succeed, financially or in life in general, is because it never occurs to them that they really can. They spend their lives re-convincing themselves that success is for the other guy and not for them. The way in which they think disqualifies them from even trying. If you're present mindset continually tells you, 'That's for others but not for me'; then it will be for others and not for you.

Successful people believe in the creative process that is at work in every individual. Unsuccessful people don't. Or, they don't believe consistently enough. They spend their time talking themselves out of the very thing they desire. As a result, they never try or don't try on a persistent enough bases for it to happen. The times it does happen in their lives, they see it as a fluke or a coincidence. They never start, so they continue to go around in the same financial circles burning a lot of rubber and creating a lot of smoke but never leaving the starting line.

You must understand that success and wealth comes to you because your thoughts and actions say that you need it and not just desire it. There are things you want to do with it. Desire alone will not help you accomplish your plans. You may have the desire to find your way around Houston but if you are using a Dallas map, it won't work. You have to get the right map or stop and ask for directions from someone who has the right information like a postal worker, cab driver, policeman, or a UPS/FEDEX driver. You need the right information the first time. Get my point?

You must demonstrate a need for wealth in all five areas by allowing all of your actions—spiritual, mental, physical, relational and financial—to align themselves up with the seeds of truth set forth in this book. Decide that you need it to fulfill your vision and dreams. These principles aren't new. Like I've already said, I'm only restating what has been said over thousands of years.

You're The Secret

When you begin to Think Big and Dream Big about your financial success, you begin to change the way you see yourself and your life. Something wonderful happens to you when you resolve and set your mind to understand and accomplish what you've set out to do no matter what. Then you make your way prosperous successful.

Use your mental gifting to begin thinking different thoughts; do different things. Let your thoughts and actions agree. Thought by thought, feeling by felling, effort by effort you will gradually change until the entire course and direction for your life completely unrecognizable by those who knew you in the past. It's like turning an ocean liner. It may take some effort but once you get it pointed in the right direction it's hard to stop because of the momentum it creates.

Your life is the same way. You must visualize before you see it materialize If you've been there in your thoughts then you can go there in your body. Dreams are the rudder that can change the course of your starship pointing it in the direction of the stars.

Chart your course. Come up with the most powerful strategy you can imagine. Put that strategy into immediate action. Take action. Take action. Take action. Dream it. Think it. Believe it. Do it. Just do it. These are a must to living a successful life. Be courageous.

SUCCESS SEED 4

Develop an Acute Sense Of Direction

"The best way to succeed is to have a specific Intent, a clear Vision, a plan of Action, and the ability to maintain Clarity. Those are the Four Pillars of Success. It never fails!"

-Steve Maraboli

What you do must be done intentionally. It must be acted upon after having the correct information at the right time. You must know what you are doing, why you are doing it and the expected outcome of your actions mentally and spiritually. Life must be lived on purpose. Life must be embraced. You must know where you are going, how to get there and be willing to pay the price it requires for the journey.

I'm sure you've heard the old saying, "he just walks around with his head in the clouds all day. 'This is the life of a true dreamer. Now don't get me wrong, I'm not suggesting there's anything wrong with being a dreamer. Nothing happens until someone dreams it and sees it. But let's face it dreams by themselves, in and of themselves, won't get it done. The combination of consistently doing the right things with the right information will help you accomplish your goals. At some point you'll have to keep your head in the clouds using your IMAGE-ENGINE while at the same time keeping your hands, feet and the rest of your body on the ground where the actions is.

You're The Secret

The eventual crystallization of your dreams must be made clear and the best way to do that is start writing them down. There's something powerful about getting it on paper. *"Write the vision down and make it plain that they may read it and run with". Habakkuk 3:3 Even* the Creator of the universe knows the power of writing it down. There is a release or allowance that takes place when you develop an acute sense of direction. Make these declarations everyday and all day long.

1. I know where I'm going.

2. I know how to get there.

3. I have a plan to get there on time.

4. I download good information daily.

5. I know how to process that information.

6. I know how to upload good information every day; everywhere to everyone I come in touch with.

7. My course is set.

8. I have set my heart and mind to understand.

9. I will self discover each day of my life.

10. I will live my life one thought at time.

Use these 10 powerful declarations every day until you recondition your thinking. Say them until they become true for you. Set the course of your mind and never look back. Change the way you see yourself and what you must do with your life. The saying still holds true today, 'You become what you think about most of the time'.

You're The Secret

The three factors that, more than anything else, determine what happens to you in life are *what* you think about, *how* you think about it and your *reaction* to what you think about. The events that take place in your life and the way you choose to respond to those events will determine your outcome. Whatever you focus on will become your reality. When you choose to focus on what you want to see happen and not what's happening, just watch the changes that begin to take place. Stop focusing on changing others and start to focus on changing you. You will discover that when you change for the better everyone around you begin to do the same.

You must learn to think about your goals constantly if you ever intend to achieve supercharged greatness success. In the beginning, it gives you a terrible headache and is probably one of the most stressful things you'll ever do. But change is vital and necessary for your success. When you continually move toward your goals, your goals continually move toward you and your purpose in the universe. The more you empower and supercharge yourself, the more you will discover the energy and vitality that draws your goals and other successful opportunities to you.

Whatever you choose to meditate on the most, will grow and increase in your life no matter what it is. If your thoughts, conversations and visualizations are on your goals, you will achieve far greater results than the average person, who thinks and talks about their worries, problems and fears or the latest thing that's gone viral on YOUTUBE™.

Discovering the true purpose of your mind is essential for your success. Your mind is fertile ground for all *kinds* of seed thoughts. It's up to you to pay attention to the kind of thoughts and the type of information you choose to allow to be planted in that fertile ground. Whatever kind of seed thoughts, words or conduct you plant in your mind will be the kind of harvest you reap.

Your mind was created to be the depository of sound thoughts and thinking to archive the tremendous and unlimited potential of your image-engine-nation of your genius. Genius is nothing more than your ability to choose what you will spend your life doing with your mind, abilities, talents and time.

Let the following eight questions assist you in re-training your mind in developing an acute sense of direction. All successful people understand, as the farmer does, that your success is in the setup. If you set it up correctly, then you will greatly benefit from your effort but if you set it up incorrectly, then you will not possess the rewards you expect and desire.

Here's eight *"IT'S IN THE SET UP"* that you can implement right now.

1. Write down what you want in each area of your life.

2. Write down what you're willing to invest and leave behind in order to accomplish your dreams.

3. Clearly write down your goals specifically outlining your course of action and strategies.

4. Set a deadline and target date for each of your goals and set sub-deadlines if the goal is big enough.

5. Make a list of everything you can think of that you will have to do to achieve each goal. As you think of new ideas, be sure to add them to your list. Be sure to stay

You're The Secret

open to your goal list changing when necessary. However, your core goals should remain consistent.

6.   Organized your list into a plan of action. Decide what you will do first and what you will do later. Decide what is more important and what is less important. Remember you can't manage time you can only manage your priorities.

7.   Take action on your plan immediately. Taking immediately action sets the course for breaking the stronghold of procrastination.

8.   Do something every waking hour of the day that moves you forward and brings you one step closer to your important goal. Start with your mind and what you download process and upload during the course of the day. This commitment to a daily course of action beginning with your thoughts will make you a huge success in whatever you want to accomplish.

Take a sheet of paper and write the word "goals" at the top of the page with today's date. Make a list of 10 goals that you would like to achieve over the next 12 months. Write your goals in the present tense; as though time has passed and you have already achieved them. Begin each goal with the word "**I**" to make it personal to you.

For example: over the past ten years I have been fortunate to achieve _____.

Do this for your 10 goals in your areas of accomplishments.

By making out a list of 10 goals for yourself for the next year, you will move yourself into an exclusive group consisting of only 3 percent of adults in our society. The sad fact is that 97 percent of adults have never written down a list of goals in their entire lives. All successful people are goal oriented and they write it all down.

You're The Secret

Once you have your list of 10 goals, go over the list and ask this key question:

Which one goal on this list, if I were to achieve it, would have the greatest positive impact on my life?

    1.   Circle that goal an make it that your number one, most important goal for the future.

    2.   Set a deadline, make a plan, take action on your plan, and do something every day that moves you toward that goal.

From now on, think and talk about that goal consistently. Think and talk about how you can achieve that goal. Think and talk about the different steps you can take to make that goal a reality. This will stimulate your creativity, increase your energy and unlock more and more of your latent potential.

SUCCESS SEED 5

Think Like An Entrepreneur & Business Owner

Son Always Own Your Own Business if You Plan to Make Any Money and Get Ahead
                                                    -Willie B. Burton, Sr.

"I got myself a start by giving myself a start"

                                                    -Madame C.J. Walker

Successful people always—I mean always—have their minds set on being an entrepreneur and business owner. It doesn't matter if they are working for someone else or not, in their minds they are working for themselves. They visualize it as being their business and they take care of what belongs to someone else as though it belonged to them.

They see employment as an opportunity to sharpen their working skills and abilities to prepare them to own their own business one day. This is why they enjoy their work so much.

The late Sam Walton, creator of the Wal-Mart empire, started out working at a Ben-Franklin Five & Dime store in Bentonville, AR. Mr. Walton put the experience he gained by working for someone else into action in his own business enterprise called Wal-Mart

You're The Secret

Successful people know how to make every job and every job position count no matter what. They will extract the gold, silver and platinum ores of opportunity from every job experience and catalog it in their minds for retrieval at a later date. They are just smart that way.

Are you one of those kinds of people? If so, then read on.

As far back as I can remember, I've been thinking like a business owner. No matter what I was doing, I always felt like I was doing it for myself. When I was in the sixth grade, I built my first dog house from scrap wood I'd collected from a nearby construction site. I hauled the wood to my house in a little red wagon tied to the back of my bike. My dad was still using that dog house when I married thirteen years.

When I was thirteen years old I rode my bicycle to the Ramada Inn about a quarter of a mile from where I lived and got my first job as a bus boy and dishwasher. I can still remember washing dishes and busing tables like that was my restaurant and everyone was working for me. I remember selling lemonade and collecting soda bottles to sell at the neighborhood store and going with my dad on Saturdays to sell metals to the salvage yard. I was a business man like my dad. My dad's success rose and fell on his own efforts.

You might say that business ownership is in my blood. I watched my father be self employed by owning his own yard contracting company starting in the late fifties and all the way through the late seventies. He started his own yard contracting business because he didn't like someone else controlling his income potential. He was determined to make his own destiny. Little did I realize that the law of transference was alive and well in watching and working alongside my dad in those yards so many years ago.

If you ever hope to arrive at your intended destination successfully, from this moment on, you must acknowledge and accept completely that you are 100 percent responsible for all that you are and all that you will ever become. Refuse to make

You're The Secret

any more excuses or blame others for your problems or shortcomings and the misfortunes that occur in your life. Hey, like the old saying says, 'into each life a little rain must fall'. So get out your umbrella and rain boots and go dance in the rain. Like they say; 'when life gives you lemons make lemonade'.

Cease all complaining about the things in your life that you can't change or have power over; for instance, other people. Stop talking about all the things you are not happy about and start speaking and being excited about what you want to happen in a positive way in your life. Criticizing others people only de-energizes you. Besides it just isn't wise. Even though what you are saying may be true, it only draws more of the same thing to you. The same energy you put out is what you will get back in return. Remember, you are responsible for what you choose to think about and meditate on.

Change your attitude to a mind and heart of gratitude. I've heard about one guy who was struggling to be grateful each day. He found a simple solution to his dilemma. He found rock in a stream on his property one morning as he was taking his morning walk and decided that he could take around with him in his pocket as a focus point to remind him of the things he had to be grateful for each day. Each time he reached into his pocket and felt the rock or took the rock out emptying his pockets each night, he would say—out loud—a series of things he was grateful for.

If you're having trouble being grateful find a rock, a marble, or something to focus your attention on that will help you remember to move your mindset to one of gratitude each day.

This is your dream, your vision. Whatever is in your life you don't like, you are responsible for and have the power of choice to change it—whatever it is. You are in charge of you. You're the Secret. Become response-able or able to respond. If you don't like the program change the challenge. Your choice.

You're The Secret

When you see yourself as self employed, you develop an entrepreneurial mindset; a mindset of a highly independent, self-responsible, self-starting individual. It literally transforms your outlook on life and everything around you. Rather than waiting for things to happen, you make things happen and encourage others to do the same. You see yourself as the owner of your own life. You see yourself as completely in charge of your spiritual, educational, physical, relational and financial wealth and well being and also that of others who have placed their confidence in you.

You are in charge of every aspect of your life, especially in choosing the way you will respond to each situation. This is the mind set of successful people. Only the top 3 percent of Americans see themselves as self-employed business owners. What that means is this. There is plenty of room at the top for you. There's always room at the top for one more. Join the ranks of those who have made the decision to pave their own way, make their own choices and write their own paychecks. Your choice.

I can remember always thinking no matter whom I was working for, feeling like I was self-employed. The biggest mistake you can ever make is to think that you work for anyone other than yourself. Whether you realize it or not you are in fact working for yourself; you just don't own the company but you do own your life which by the way is the only real company. That is your company. Your company is contracting you out to another company to do the work as agreed upon for a certain sum of money called a paycheck. Like it or not, you are the president and CEO of your own personal contract service corporation; no matter where you might be working or who you are working for at the moment.

A self-responsible person is always looking for the best results. They have a strong sense of seeing a job well done and will not be satisfied with anything less. They always take high levels of initiative. They will be the first to volunteer for assignments and are always asking for more responsibility. Because of this, they

You're The Secret

are able to increase their value and net worth on a consistent basis.

Even if where they are working doesn't acknowledge their true worth, they know it's just a matter of time before the universe will expose them directly to better opportunities whether with someone else or on their own. Every effort is performed with this understanding. They are investing in their present and future. They know that opportunity will always seek them out, find them and reward them for their excellent efforts.

These are the respected ones in their organizations. These are the ones that everyone is whispering and talking about. These are the movers, game changers and the innovators. These are the ones who have what it takes to move the minds of men and companies forward toward even greater summits of success and stellar performances.

The real fear of success is not to have tried and failed and become fearful of ever trying again. It's the fear of what price you will have to pay in effort and time to succeed. In other words how much of your life you have to invest to see your dreams manifest and succeed?

Successful people understand that visible success comes at a price and they have counted up the cost and determined they have are willing to do what must be done to start and finish the course. They understand that victory loves preparation and are in a constant state of preparedness; always ready to embrace new positions of greater influence, authority and responsibility thereby casting their vision into the future. What if you did the same? Your choice.

SUCCESS SEED 6

Do What You Love; Love What You Do

When You Begin Doing What You Love to Do,
You Align Yourself With the
Divine Beauty and Order of All Creation
                                    -Donald W. Burton

It's already done. The universe is waiting for you to pay
attention to what your core—or the voice of your *Innerman*—is
saying to you in order to carry your dreams forward. It's waiting
to burst forth in your life like flowers in the spring. But, you
have to release it because you're the secret. You won't find truly
successful people doing what they don't love to do. The set up
has already been staged and scripted. All you need do is
recognize, acknowledge and receive the seed planted within you
from the beginning. It's time you get actively involved in your
future.

Aligning yourself with what has already been done and
completed for you and on your behalf is paramount to your
success in life both now and in the future. Successful people
understand this principle. They may not know what to call it but
they are aware of it and they use it quite effectively in their daily
lives. Some people call it a stroke of good luck or a stroke of
genius when things work in their favor. To their good, however,
they begin to notice over time that when they do things in a
certain way they consistently have the same 'stroke of luck'
come their way. So is it a stroke of luck or is it the ability to
discover what works over and over again in order to get the
same successful results?

You're The Secret

That's when they discover it was never about luck but about knowledge, getting the right information and knowing how to make that information work on your behalf with the application of appropriate action.

Successful people know that there's absolutely no fulfillment in doing what you don't like to do. So, they've made the decision to stop doing what they don't like and concentrate all of their energy like a powerful laser beam onto what they loved to do. They know they can't always do it immediately so they gradually begin to move toward in that direction and do what they want and steadily wean themselves from what they no longer wish to do. But they always make sure they finish strong where they already are first. You can make that decision TODAY as well!

One of the primary responsibilities in life is to find out what you truly enjoy doing. Ask yourself, what do I have a natural talent for? Whatever that is, take all that you are—known and unknown, seen and unseen—into doing that particular work extremely well. There's no greater feeling than discovering what you really love to do and doing it every day of your life, for the rest of your life. This is one of the amazing discoveries of highly successful people.

Successful people are those who have discovered a field of endeavor where their natural core strengths and abilities are exactly what are required to do the job and accomplish the results they want. You'll hear most successful people claim they've 'never worked a day in their lives'. Why? Because when you're doing what you love and love what you're doing, your days of merely working for a pay check are over and done. It's time to **MYFL...** *"Move Your Life Forward!*

It's imperative that you find a field in which you can be totally absorbed, that you can lose yourself in. Find an opportunity or endeavor that completely fascinates , invigorates and holds your attention, something that is a natural expression of your core talents and core abilities.

You're The Secret

Find an opportunity that demands that you do your best, be your best and perform at your best every day. That's called Real Living.

When you are doing what you love and love what you're doing, you produce a different energy, power and flow of constant enthusiasm that others quickly are drawn to. There's an excitement, an energetic exuberance and a deluge of ideas and creativity that makes what you want to share it with others. Ask yourself. If someone wrote you a check for a million dollars would you keep doing what you're doing right now or would you change dance partners as soon as possible?

Hey, it's a fair question don't you think? I'm simply asking what you would do if you had all the time and money you required and were free to choose any occupation or endeavor you wanted to. What would that occupation look like, feel like and how would it change your life for the better? In the words of a one successful individual, 'If I won a million dollars I wouldn't change a thing, I'd keep doing what I'm doing only on a higher level'. This is when you know you're doing what you love. Successful people love what they do so much that they wouldn't even consider leaving it or retiring from it no matter how much money they were given. They'd just find a way to do more of it with the additional capital.

In my opinion possibly one of the greatest challenges in life, whether you're in high school, college or an adult, is to take time and discover what you really love to do and not be afraid to find out what it really is. What is that one thing that makes you light up on the inside just thinking about it, that gets you excited and your blood pumping just talking to others about it. Take a long hard look at it and face it in the mirror of your mind and start doing something about it as you move your life forward. It's "That Thing" that never goes away or comes and goes but it's always there.

Then ask yourself is this one of your core desires? Spend some time by yourself and asking hard questions like, what kind of person do I want to be? How would I like for others to

You're The Secret

remember me? How do I wish to be spoken of in conversations in my absence? What do I really love doing and then commit and dedicate yourself to that endeavor. You're the only one who can do this for you. If you don't have the skill set and training to do it right now, formulate a plan of action, go get the right information then take the appropriate action steps find out what should be done. NOW!

SUCCESS SEED 7

To Be Excellent Is A Choice, Choose Well

Aim for the Highest

-Andrew Carnegie

Do Not Look For Approval Except,

For The Consciousness Of Doing Your Best.

-Andrew Carnegie

As I've stated before success seeds are already in you. Much like all of the beautiful flowers that come out every spring, you must acquaint or reacquaint yourself with the seeds of greatness lying dormant in you at this very moment. From underneath cold frigid temperatures to mild ones, these flowers will bloom and dress the planet with dazzling displays of colors that will leave us spell bound and inspired. No human can take credit for these wonders of nature and no human can take credit the wonders that lie waiting within them to be discovered. All we can do is sit back and enjoy the show. Success seeded inside of you in the very same way and it's time you start to do something about it.

Excellence happens to be one of those amazing seeds. Resolve today to be the very best at what you do, what you say and who you are. With this right mental attitude, set a goal for yourself to join the top 10 percent of like minded men and women in your

You're The Secret

chosen profession. This decision, to become extremely good at what you do, can be the turning point in your life. Virtually all successful people are recognized as being extremely competent in their chosen fields and profession. This is not by accident but intentional. I'm sure you've noticed that when someone in authority wants an opinion they first find out who is considered the expert in that field. There's usually someone who has done more research and clocked more hours and effort than anyone else.

Remember, no one is better than you and no one is smarter than you. And vice versa, you're no better than or smarter than anyone else. They have simply developed a life style of doing things in a very specific and intentional way every day. The playing field is level. Everyone who is in the top 10 percent of their field today started off in the bottom 10 percent at one time. Everyone who is doing well was once doing very poorly. Everyone who is at the top of his or her field was one time in another field altogether.

What countless others have done, you can do as well. In other words, if they can do it so can you. No one starts in a place of excellence and being an expert in their field. It must be earned through the same hard work and effort everyone else has to do. It's like I said before, most people are not willing to pay the price in the effort and sacrifices required to become excellent.

Here is a great rule for success: Your life only gets better when you want it to get better. Your opportunities will increase when you want them to increase. Your bottom line will increased when you are willing to do what it takes for it to increase.

You will awaken yourself to success when you choose to diligently apply the truths that will awaken you to the reality of who you are and what you should do. There is no limit to how much better you can become or how success you can be. The more you know the more there is to know. The more you achieve the more you will find to achieve. In the final analysis, it's your choice to make your life as exciting as you want it to be. You're the Secret.

Your decision to become excellent at what you do, to join the top 10 percent in your field, will be the turning point in your life. It's the key to all great success stories. It is also the foundation of high levels of self-esteem, self-respect, and a valuable source of personal pride and yes even financial wealth. Join the ranks of those who are trusted as a source of great information that is accurate and precise. Financial wealth is what you receive for helping someone solve their problem(s). People are always ready to give you money if you are able to help them solve their problem. That's why they came to you in the first place.

When you're really good at what you do, you feel wonderful about yourself. Being excellent affects your entire existence, your personality changes for the better. You discover that you are never stuck with the person or personality you were born with or conditioned by through the environment you grew up in. When you chose to be excellent, everything and everyone around you recognizes it. Relationships improve and you feel happy and proud when you know you are at the top of your field. People and success are naturally drawn to the excellence and virtue you show. It is the order of the universe. Everybody appreciates respect and for a job well done.

You cannot become good at everything right away, but you can identify the one core skills that can help you the most and then throw your whole heart, soul and mind into developing that skill. Set a goal. Write it down. Set a deadline. Make a plan. Set a course of action today. Work on becoming better in that area every single day. You will be absolutely amazed at the difference this commitment to excellence will make in your life. This commitment to excellence alone can make you a truly successful person.

Ask yourself: What one skill, if developed and done in an excellent way, would have the greatest positive impact on my life today? What are the things that fascinate me with childlike wonder.

SUCCESS SEED 8

Work Harder & Work Longer
But Work Smarter

You Had Better Learn How To Use Your Mind.

Your Back Will Play Out

Long Before Your Mind Will.

-Willie B. Burton Sr.

Wishing to own lands and cattle, to have nice clothes and money in your wallet and being willing to work hard for it isn't enough. Even your willingness to work with all the strength in your body and with all the skill of your hands and the cunning of your mind, in and of itself is not enough. You must learn and apply the wisdom of those who are financially succeeding where you are financially failing. These individuals are all around. You must discover what they do each day and the principles they've learned to habitually apply to every aspect of their lives. It doesn't cost anything to get advice from someone who's already doing what you're thinking about doing.

My dad had a saying; "You'd better learn how to use your mind and not just your back. Because your back will play out long before your mind will". 'He was absolutely right about that. I was fortunate to watch my dad do both quite well. He knew how to use his mind and back extremely well and the result of that combination was watching poetry in motion. He knew how to turn manual labor into an adventure. Hard work alone will not make you successful or wealthy. It just makes you tired, exhausted, irritable and worn out. However, working longer and harder will serve you well provided you discover the art of working smarter as well. Your mind is the key to effective work and results.

Find in yourself a new energy, drive and intensity and joy in completing every task you're given. Rediscover the joy of saying to yourself, "job well done" or "I love it when a plan comes together".

Before we go any further into this chapter I think we need a working definition of what I mean by 'work'. Let me begin by explaining what work is not. Work is not getting up before sunrise and going to bed in the wee hours of the night only to get up and do the same thing again. It's not the back breaking work performed for someone else and the only thing you get for it is an eight to five pay check. All this is fine and well for a season but unfortunately it will not go very far in helping you on your quest to business ownership.

The kind of hard work that I refer to is the kind that involves your mind first, your passion second and your body last. I call it the one, two, three punch. It's the kind of work that challenges you to know why you're getting up early and staying up late and putting that kind of effort into serving someone else. You know that there's an end in sight. So your labor is no longer in vain. This type of work demands you have a plan and purpose with specific results in mind that goes beyond a paycheck or some other fringe benefit. It demands that you keep your brain involved all of the time. If you are sluggish and lazy minded trust me opportunities for success will elude you at every turn. Opportunity seeks out those individuals who have prepared themselves to take advantage of opportunity when it presents itself. If you are not prepared for opportunity it will quickly bypass you and present itself to someone who has prepared themselves for her. Opportunity loves to keep company with those who are prepared. Opportunity demands that your plan

You're The Secret

includes the possibility for advancement in your profession. If not with your present company it will be with another one or maybe with your own. Either way you will win. Opportunity will make sure of it provided you are ready when it comes knocking.

All successful people work longer, harder and smarter than everyone else. They understand how important it is to put the necessary energy and drive into the setup. For example, let's use the farmer again. Years ago I had the privilege of living in a farming and ranch community. Every farmer knows that if he doesn't do the clearing, plowing, planting and irrigating the soil his chances of a bumper crop when it's time for the harvest are next to none.

His personal experiences and the combined experiences combined with the transference of knowledge from past generations of farmers from all over the world tell him that the success is in the setup. You can't expect to get something from something you haven't properly setup. The farmer knows he has a greater chance of reaping a great harvest if he puts forth the hard work and the smart work in the right season. It works the same with whatever you're planning to do. Your success will be greater if you take time to set it up correctly the first.

Success minded people know that if they don't work longer, harder and smarter their dreams will never be realized. So, they do what is necessary in order to see the birth of their ideas and the acquisition of wealth. It's like a guy I use to work for always said, 'if you everything the right way, the money just has a way of just being there' and he was absolutely right.

Who plants a garden, takes care of it, keeps the insects and animals away from it, waters it every day and expecting not eat from the very garden they planted?

And so it is with wealth. If you do the things you need to, when you need to do them in a persistent certain way; you will reap the financial rewards of your effort. The universe will see to it.

You're The Secret

I read this in a book once. Practice the "40 Plus" formula. This formula says that you work 40 hours per week for survival; everything over 40 hours per week is for success. If you work only 40 hours (and the average workweek today is closer to 35 hours), all you are doing is surviving. You will never get ahead. You will never be a financial success. You will never be highly respected and esteemed by your colleagues. You will stay at level of mediocrity working the basic 40-hour week.

But every hour over 40 hours, you are investing in your future. In fact, you can tell with pin-point accuracy exactly where you are going to be in five years by looking at how many hours over 40 you put in every week. There's no substitute for longs days, hard work and smarter work.

Successful people in America work in average of 59 hours per week. Many of them work 70 or 80 hours, especially at the start of their careers. They put in the extra time when they are younger and stronger. They work an average of six days per week, rather than five, and work longer days as well.

If you want to call a successful person, phone the office before normal working hours or after normal working hours. Successful people are there when the staff, the 'nine-to-fivers' and the called in because 'I don't feel good today folk', arrive and are still there when they leave. The story is told of Michael Jordan that he was always in the gym before everyone else and still in the gym after everyone had left shooting hundreds of baskets. The rest is basketball and sports history.

Here's the key: **When you work make sure you work**.

Let me say that again. When you work make sure you work. When you work, don't waste time. When you get in early, check your assignments and get started immediately. When people want to talk to you, excuse yourself and say, "I have to get back to work!" Be gracious and considerate but get back to work. It's difficult to master this skill because our culture encourages us to get by with doing as little as possible and still expect to be compensated for work we've not done. In our society we want

You're The Secret

to reap the most for very little productivity and feel good about the fact that at least we showed up on time to punch the clock.

Don't drop off your dry cleaning, phone or text your friends, socialize with your coworkers, or read the newspaper or magazine. Heaven forbid if you are wasting time on a social network online.

Work all the time you are at work! Resolve today to develop the skills and reputation for being the hardest working person in your company. The famous entertainer of the 1970's James Brown was billed as being the "hardest working man in show business".

When your company comes looking for solutions and great information and believe me they will, let your name be the name that's mentioned first and foremost. This will bring you to the attention of people who can help you move forward faster than almost anything else you can do. I call this the law of acceleration or time collapsing. Some choose to call them miracles. Knowledge is power. Choose knowledge.

Society is full of people who are content the doing enough to maintain the status quo. And please understand if that's what you would like to do with your life then by all means have at it. BUT if you plan on reaching a level of success and sustained wealth in your life you'll have to do things in a different way.

People of excellence have no desire in maintaining the status quo. They're different. They march to a different drummer and dance to a different groove. They move to the internal rhythms and melodies hear and create within themselves.

These people are always smiling and cheerful. They don't wait for the band to show up to start the concert. They bring the band and the concert with them because they are the band.

Your mind and what you choose to do with it is your ticket to personal success and financial freedom.

You're The Secret
SUCCESS SEED 9

Be A Forever Life Learner

Formal education will get you a job,

Self education will make you wealthy

-Jim Rohm

Every person possesses the unlimited capacity to learn, improve and grow in order to release their success. This translates into huge relational, financial and wealth benefits for you both now and in the future. You have more brains, ability, and intelligence than you could ever use if you commit to lifelong personal growth and development

. You are literally a manufacturing plant of creativity and unharnessed ideas and possibilities.

You are smarter than you can even begin to imagine. There is no obstacle that you cannot overcome, no problem you cannot solve, and no goal you cannot achieve by applying the power of your mind and heart to your situation. The combination of observation, self-education and application works every time and in every situation.

Your mind is a muscle that develops only with use. Just as you have to strain your physical muscles to build them, you have to work your mental muscles to build your mind as well.

The art of meditation is a powerful proven way to achieve greater control over the creative processes of your mind. The good news is that the more you learn, the more you can learn.

You're The Secret

Just like the more you play a sport, the better you get at the sport. As a matter of fact the more you do anything in life, the more you can do of that particular thing; good or bad, right or wrong the principle is still the same. You develop a greater skill set or ability for whatever you're doing the more you do a thing in a certain way. The more you dedicate yourself to lifelong learning practices, the easier it is for you to learn more about life and living.

All leaders are forever learners. You'll continuously find them reading, learning and discovering more than they knew the day before. They're normally reading at least ten books or more on various subject during the course of a week. Continuous learning is the key to true and lasting success.

Forever life learning is the minimum requirement for success in any field. Become an in your field by becoming Forever Learner for the rest your life. Practice in your mind the outcomes you would like to see. Visualize yourself doing the same type of activities that you read of other accomplishing. Practices this every day until you are able to experience it yourself.

There are three keys to Forever Life learning:

ONE: Read good informational books, publications, essays, research and reports in your field for at least 30 to 60 minutes each day. *READING IS TO THE MIND & SOUL WHAT EXERCISE IS TO THE BODY.* You need to put good information in your mind every day and all day if you ever expect to cancel out and help detoxify and replace the wrong information you're bombarded with during the day. Wrong information only serves to undermine your success strategies and paralyzes the implementation of your plans.

You're The Secret

Depending on the length of the book, reading for an hour a day translates into about one book per week. Set aside the time you need to read. View it as a part of your working smarter plan. One book per week will translate into 50 books per year. Fifty books per year will translate into 500 books over the next 10 years. 500 books over the next ten years of your life will place you into that 10 percentile of people who are experts in their chosen professions.

Since the average adult reads less than one book per year, when you begin reading an hour per day, one book per week will give you an incredible edge in your field. You will become one of the smartest, most competent, and highest paid people in your professional by simply reading one hour each day. Remember what I said earlier money is what you receive when you help someone solve a problem. Becoming knowledgeable in you chosen profession will position you helping people solve their problems.

And don't forget about adding one new word to your vocabulary each day. This comes to an amazing increase of 3,650 words in your vocabulary in ten short years. I'm sure some who reads this will ask, why bother? I'll be ten years older by the time I read that many books and memorize that many words? The fact of the matter is, in 10 years you're going to be that much older anyway. You may as well use the time to become an expert in your profession. People never succeed because they never start doing those certain things in a certain way that creates success.

TWO: Commit to a learning life style by listening to audio programs in your car as your drive from place to *palace*. That was not a misspelled word. I meant to say palace. Success will put you in the *palace* or better yet build your own palace, provided you stay true to your course of conduct and action. In the course of a 40 to 60 hour work week you will spend 500 to 1,000 hours per year behind the wheel of your car. This is the

You're The Secret

equivalent of 12 to 24 forty-hour work weeks, or as much as 3 to 6 months of working time spent in your car: time you don't get paid for. This is the same amount of time you would spend attending one to two full-time semesters as a university student.

That's a lot of drive time that can never be regained. The most valuable commodity on the planet is time. It's the only thing you can't get any more of. Every person receives a ration of twenty-four hours each day. It's how they choose to prioritize that will determine their level of success.

So, while you may not be able to manage time you can however manage your priorities. One of your priorities should be to effectively use that drive time in your vehicle.

Turn your car into a learning mobile university, your own private tutor, your own personal professor and life coach on wheels. Your car motor should never be running without an educational audio program playing. Many people have become millionaires through the miracle of audio learning. Knowledge is power and power is that unexplainable, inexhaustible life force that is ever unfolding and ever increasing.

Take advantage of the knowledge you're accumulating in the privacy of your automobile. This is why audio learning is often considered the greatest breakthrough in education since the invention of the printing press. It gives you the opportunity to go one on one with some of the most incredible leaders of your day.

THREE: Try to attend every course and seminar you can find that will help you better in yourself in your field.

The powerful 1,2,3 combination punch of books, audio programs, and seminars will enable you to save hundreds of hours, thousands of dollars, and many years of hard work and trial and error in achieving the level of financial success you desire. This is probably the most powerful way to time collapse and accelerate time known to man outside of supernatural intervention of course.

Through the benefit of technology, opportunities to acquire knowledge are faster thank ever. And with the advent of hand held devices and eBooks with more on the way there's really no excuse for you to not know what you need to know.

But it's still up to you to decide what you will do with the knowledge. No amount of technology and learning can make you apply what you claim to know. This is what separates those who are successful from those who enjoy talking about success but never experience it. Most people think that because they know about it they've done it. Let me say that again. *Most people think that because they know about it they've done it.* It's called false experience. You can't build a successful life on the experiences of other people. Just because you see your favorite sports star do some incredible things on television doesn't qualify you to be able to accomplish the same feats.

The difference is they're paid the price in conditioning their mind and body to do that and you haven't. So your experience would be called a "false experience".

Make a decision today to become a forever life learner. You will amaze yourself at the effect that it has on your career. Write your decision down. Sign and date it then make the commitment to do it. LifeLong learning is a major factor in your becoming a truly successful person.

SUCCESS SEED 10

Pay Yourself First

"A Part Of All You Earn Is Yours To Keep".
"Money Is Plentiful For Those Who Understand
The Simple Rules Of Its Acquisition"
The Richest Man in Babylon by George S. Clason

What a powerful statement of truth. Before you will ever be trusted with wealth, you must first demonstrate that you have placed the correct value on its acquisition. People will never trust you with their money if you haven't been responsible with your own money. Until you do this, financial wealth will always avoid you. The discipline and practice of saving a part of all you earn is a powerful place to begin because anyone can do it. Even Ants know this fundamental rule. Below are some power plays, suggestions and action steps that will help you on your way to financial freedom.

1. Increase your balance in your savings account.

2. Whenever you get a raise don't spend it save it.

3. Save ten percent of your yearly tax returns.

4. Control what you spend.

5. For every dollar you spend make it a point to earn five times as much and more. In other words if you spend 1 dollar you should earn five to ten dollars to replace it.

You're The Secret

6. Make your dollars multiply with savings and investments.

7. Protect your mind and your money from loss and lack.

8. Find inexpensive ways to increase the profitability of your home.

9. Make wise precise choices to insure you have income in the future.

10. Discover and increase your ability to earn more income through the use of your imagination and creativity and not just by working harder.

11. Discover methods to draw wealth and success to you. Just make sure you're prepared for it.

12. It's not about greed; it's about the need to succeed.

13. Everything around you is constantly moving forward. Pay attention to the direction that life is going.

14. Whatever you ignore, abuse, disrespect or not pay attention or value will exit your life. If you don't value money enough to save and learn to invest it wisely it will either exit your life or avoid you completely.

15. Set your Mind and Heart to know that you are going to save and invest at least 10 percent of your income throughout your working life and beyond. This is part of working smarter; not just harder and longer philosophy.

16. Teach your children and grandchildren to do the same.

17. Take 10 percent of your income off the top of your paycheck and put it into a special account for the sole

You're The Secret

purpose of financial accumulation. If you save just $100 per month throughout your working lifetime and invest that money in an average mutual fund that grows at 10 percent per annum, you will be worth more than one million dollars by the time you retire depending on how early you begin your savings program.

18. Anyone—even a person earning minimum wage—if they start early enough and consistently contributes to saving, can become a millionaire over the course of their working lifetime.

19. The acquisition of money is plentiful for those who understand the simple rules of acquiring it.

20. Developing a life style or habit of saving and investing your money is not easy. It requires tremendous determination, discipline and will power.

21. Set it as a goal, write it down, make a plan, and work on it all the time and run with it. Once these proactive habits lock in and become automatic, your financial success is virtually assured.

22. Overtime you will start to experience the amazing law of accumulation.

23. You will have moved yourself into a state of conscientiousness that draws wealth and opportunities your way very naturally and serves you because you now know and understand the purpose for its acquisition.

24. Practice the art of frugality, frugality, frugality in all things. Be very careful with every penny. You should question expenditures you're thinking of making. Delay

or defer every important buying decision for at least a week, if not a month. The longer you put off making a buying decision, the better your decision will be. Chances are they will have a better model at a less expensive price if you prolong your purchase.

25. Impulse buying is a major reason people retire poor, broke and dependent upon social programs, families and similar programs. They see something they like and they buy it with very little thought. They become victims of what is called "Parkinson's Law" which says that 'expenses rise to meet income'. This means that no matter how much you earn, you spend that much and a little bit more besides. You will never get ahead and you never get out of debt with this mind set.

26. You don't have to be a victim of Parkinson's Law. If you cannot save 10 percent of your income, start today by saving 1 percent of your income in a special savings and investment account. If you have to start by putting it in an envelope or simply starting a small account at a credit union, do it. Whatever you decide to do, you must demonstrate that you have placed the proper value on financial wealth accumulation.

27. There is a universal principle at work here I just don't know what to call it yet.

28. Wealth accumulation is a dynamic that cannot be ignored. Pay yourself even before you begin paying down your debts. Live on the other 99 or 90 percent of your income perhaps even less if you can. When you start keeping accurate accounts of your income and expenditures you will be surprised how many of your expenses are completely unnecessary.

You're The Secret

29. As you become comfortable living on 99 percent, raise your saving level to 2 percent of your income, then 3 percent, 4 percent, and so on. There is something powerful about getting started and disciplining yourself to maintain a true course of change by your new actions.

30. You will find the base for all debt is greed, impatience and pleasure. People who are in debt constantly fall prey to self gratification by satisfying their pleasures at the expense of their future prosperity. They convince themselves that if they don't get it now someone else will beat them to it and they will lose out on that opportunity.

31. If you develop and implement a savings strategy, within one year you can be saving 10 percent (maybe 15 or 20) of your income and living comfortably on the balance. At the same time, your savings and investment account will grow. The longest journey begins with first step.

32. The fattest bank accounts begin with the first dollar saved and invested.

When you become more careful about your expenditures, your debts will begin to be paid off and eventually disappear completely. Within a year or two, your entire financial life will be under your control and you will be on your way to becoming a self-made success story and creating personal wealth. This process has worked for everyone who's ever tried it. Try it. See for yourself.

Wealth will always be drawn to those who know what to do with it to increase its value.

SUCCESS SEED 11

Develop the Mind and Heart
Of An Expert in Your
Business Profession

"Never become so much of an expert that you stop gaining expertise.

View life as a continuous learning experience."

-Denis Waitley

As I've already stated, Knowledge is Power. People will always pay you and pay you well to help them solve their problems. Knowledge is the result of accumulating right information over time combining with it the ability to process and effectively utilize that information through persistent experience. So it only stands to reason that your level of expertise in your field will be compensated accordingly. The marketplace pays excellent rewards for excellent performances by those who have chosen to be experts in their profession or field of engagement. The same market will only pay average rewards for average performances and below-average rewards and so forth. The greater effort you put into understanding the system will be matched by the greater reward you receive from the system. You must learn the system(s) of the universe and learn it well.

The universe responds exactly in direct proportion to what you do. It's always forward in its movements and nonstop in its progression of success. It's never later or early because it works outside of what we define as time.

You're The Secret

If you want to fly a kite you have to get facing the wind and get your back against the wind and let the wind blow in the face of the kite. Soon the kite will be soaring high up above you in the sky. If you will have success you must learn to face all opposition and resistance that will surely come your way.

Your goal, therefore, should be to be an expert in your chosen field of endeavor by learning and paying attention to every detail of how to do your work better and more effectively and efficiently.

Show me a person who is excellent in what he does and always striving for that mark. The world will pay him whatever price he chooses just to have the opportunity to see him in action and simply to be in his presence.

If you are a skilled expert in what you do you will have untold opportunities for advancement that the average person only thinks about. People will sometimes label you as the bosses pet. And I suppose that's ok in a way. Because every employer is actively looking for someone who knows how to make them money and themselves as well. You'll just have to learn how to handle the "downside" of your success as well.

Expert skills and abilities will always be recognized by those who need you to solve a problem for them and they will pay you for your expertise.

As I said earlier, read all the magazines in your field. Read and study the latest books. Attend courses and seminars given by experts in your field. Join your industry or trade associations, attend every meeting, and get involved with the other top people in your field. Join chat rooms online and see what new discoveries are being made in your field and what people are saying in real time. Start a blog and get input from other experts as well as novices. Sometimes innovation comes from the most unlikely sources and the most unlikely people. Do what is necessary to continue LifeLearning process as you gain the knowledge and experience needed to succeed.

You're The Secret

The Law of Integrative Complexity says that the individual who can integrate, connect, combine and use the greatest amount of information in any field and across fields soon rises to the top of his field.

That's just a clever way of saying that if you can take everything you know and put it into a workable format and apply the right action in a way that will help people solve their problems, you will receive a great deal of money and respect for it.

If you are in sales, become an aggressive, lifelong student of the selling process. The top 20 percent of salespeople earn, on average, 16 times the amount earned by the bottom 80 percent. The top 10 percent of salespeople earn even more.

If you are in management, set your mind to become an outstanding professional manager and watch people fight over the opportunity to employ you. If you are starting your own business, study entrepreneurial strategies and marketing tactics and try out new ideas every single day. Become a *detective* in your field.

Set your mind to become the very best in your business or profession. It only takes one small detail, insight, or idea to be the turning point in your career. Never stop looking for it. Within you lay untold levels of treasure screaming for your undivided attention to be discovered and mined from the vast deposits of your creative genius. Dig deep, dig long and dig smart.

Your choice.

SUCCESS SEED 12

Dedicate Yourself to Completing & Serving Others

A business absolutely devoted to service will have only one worry about profits. They will be embarrassingly large.

-Henry Ford

Have you ever eaten at a restaurant where you received poor service and poor food? You wanted to make sure none of your friends your friends would never go there, right? Have you ever been to a restaurant and received amazing service and amazing food? You wanted to become their star evangelist, right?

In today's society, as hectic as it is, it's still much better to give than receive. *Give and it will be given back to you in good measure pressed down shaken together and running over shall men give back to you. Luke 6:38.* That's what the great book says. And it still rings true today.

Your rewards in life will always be in direct proportion to your level of service you give to other people. All successful people have an obsession with customer service and providing amazing performances to their clients. They are continually looking for new and better ways to lead their industry in increased and improved customer service. Find innovative ways to communicate with your customers and show them what it feels like to received an amazing performance.

You're The Secret

Here are a few questions you should ask yourself on a regular basis.

1.   Who are my customers?

2.   What do my customers really want?

3.   What do my customers really need?

4.   What do my customers consider value?

5.   What can I give my customers better than anyone else?

6.   Why are my customers buying from others today and what would I have to offer them to get them to buy from me?

If you only do what you are expected to do then you should only get what you were expected to get. If you give sensational customer service you may not get it back from the customer you gave it to but I can guarantee you that you will get it from another customer in ways that will more than compensate you for your previous effort. It all goes back to what I said earlier. You have to work harder, longer and smarter and always stay vigilant for opportunities to do more than your customers have paid for. Always look for ways to increase your level of service for your customers and clients.

Remember, there are never any traffic jams on the extra mile. Always go the extra mile.

Your customers are people whom you depend on for your success in your work. This means that your boss and coworkers are customers as well as the people who buy your products or services. Your customers are also those people who depend on you for their success or satisfaction. Your job is to start a raging fire of customer satisfaction that burns out of control. Turn

You're The Secret

your customers into screaming evangelists because of the way you serve them.

Think of ways to set a fire storm among your customers and potential customers. Find ways to invest in the lives of your customers, friends, family and those who can't give anything back to you but thank you.

But even if you don't get a thank you, invest in their lives anyway. Fuel and fan the flames around you by dedicating yourself to effective service on all levels.

Here is the question that you need to answer every single day: ***What can I do to increase the value service to customers?***

People will always be drawn to what they perceive to have value and worth because it makes them feel like they have that same value and worth.

Look for ways to keep increasing and adding value to what you do and to the people who depend on you every single day. One small improvement in the way you serve your customers can be a major reason for your financial success. Never stop looking for those small ways to improve your customer's services.

All too often, other businesses overlook this. They seem to be of the mindset that "if you build it they will come". While that may work initially, I can assure you that it will not sustain you for very long. At the end of the day people are looking for the perfect blend of product, pricing, panache, performance from you.

Capitalize on their lack of vision in your business by improving your service.

Today your customer values speed and accuracy more than ever while still demanding quality and great pricing. Precision is the new world order. Those who have the right information in their possession combined with the acute sensibility to implement that information in a systematic way the first time will be the ones able to satisfy the increasing demands of savvy customers and clients.

Whenever a customer asks for anything, you should say, 'sure, right away', 'I can do that for you' or 'I'd be more than happy to get that for you' "Let me see what I can do".

These are the sweetest words that customers crave to hear. Remember customers are addicted to respect through quality service and amazing performances. Those words say that you care—and you care a lot. Just make sure you follow through with what you say.

Try creating your own arsenal of power words and phrases to let people know that you genuinely care about giving them amazing service. Practice these words and phrases on your own time until you become absolutely comfortable with them.

Implement the 'Plus One' Rule that says, "find one more thing you can say or do to strengthen your service to your client".

SUCCESS SEED 13

Be Totally Honest
With Yourself & Others

To Thine Own Self Be True
                                    -William Shakespeare

Knowledge begins with thought. All that is known has been known by someone before. In order for man to continue to survive and thrive, knowledge must be transferred intact from one generation to another. One slip in the transference of this knowledge would be catastrophic to all civilization as we know it today and possibly throw civilization back into pre-barbarianism.

The transference of wealth on all five levels—spiritual, educational, physical, relational and financial ensures the ongoing and continued success of mankind. Because of this transference, all endeavors will continue to thrive and maintain a harmonious balance on this planet and in the universe.

Therefore it is imperative that you consider as a part of your wealth building strategy, the subject of integrity. When I say integrity, I'm not only referring to paying your bills on time— which is very important of course or of keeping your word— which is equally important. I'm also talking about the responsibility you have to the very society and system that makes it possible for you to accumulate untold levels of wealth and achievement through honoring and valuing it the universal system.

You're The Secret

When you transfer the success principles you learn to others it a leaves a legacy that will outlive you and keep your name on the lips and in the center of discussions for centuries to come. Consider the names that still come to mind years after the actual person is gone: The Ford Foundation, The Rockefeller Foundation, The Andrew Carnegie Foundation and The Rothschild Foundation and many more.

The Scrooges of the world are ill remembered.

Whether through a lecture, a book, a seminar or your parents, someone was strategically placed in your life to help you achieve your success and this will continue to happen for the rest of your life; be it another human being, the universe or nature itself. We must, therefore, resolve to give back in ways what has been given to us by leaving an enduring legacy of transference in the five areas of wealth building.

Life is not to be lived one day at a time or one second at a time for that matter but rather life is to be lived one thought at a time.
-Donald W. Burton

All successful people understand this truth about thought. Thoughts are where you draw your power and strength from. Thoughts require good, accurate and correct information to fuel them and keep them focused on your goals. Your thoughts will make you or break you. They will either place you in the pit, the prison, or the palace. Thoughts travel faster than time or the speed of light. They can be where you are not; create worlds only imagined in the minds of men and never seen by the eyes of men. Your IMAGE-ENGINE-NATION is the most powerful tool you have in your possession.

Perhaps the most valued, respected and lasting quality you can develop is a reputation for absolute integrity. The Great Book states that a "good name is to be desired more than gold or silver". And while this is difficult to achieve, it's by no means impossible. Simply start by deciding to be perfectly honest in

You're The Secret

everything you do and in every transaction and activity. Never allowing desperation, fear or rejection to cause you to compromise your integrity or someone else's for that matter. At the end of the day a good name is really all you have. Your good name will create opportunities for you when your money and influence won't.

Remember money is not the answer for everything. It's only what you get for helping someone solve their problem. But it is not the problem solver. You are the solver of problems and you get paid a great deal of money for doing so. Your integrity is priceless and should be guarded as one of your most valued possessions.

I have discovered over the years that people are really looking for lasting relationships based on mutual trust and lasting friendships. It is one of the basic laws of human nature. People really want to trust other people. But people make it hard to trust other people a great deal of the time.

Seek out people who are trustworthy in their dealings with others and develop relationships with them if you are able to do so. Keep in mind that you only want to be connected to those people that you have a connection with and that's not with everybody. Always keep your eyes open to this dynamic.

All successful people and businesses are based on trust. There has to be a certain degree of honesty even among thieves. Your efforts in becoming a successful person will be determined solely by the number of people who trust you and who are willing to work for you, give you credit, lend you money, buy your products/services, and help you during difficult times.

Your character is the most important asset that you will develop in your entire life. It is based on the amount of integrity you practice daily. The key word here is practice. If this is something you haven't been good at in the past, then today is a good day to begin. Your choice.

You're The Secret

Here are a few keys for you to use in unlocking the seeds of integrity in your life:

Be true to yourself, in all things at all times. Especially when no one is looking. Like William Shakespeare said, "To thine own self be true."

Be true beyond what you think you're capable of. Set a standard for yourself that very few people would dare to imitate except those who are like minded and of similar character.

Being true to yourself means doing what you do in an excellent fashion regardless of what others do.

Integrity is the outward manifestation of inward self education and inward transformation. In other words, the world has the opportunity to see what you are diligently working on one thought at time from the inside out. Through personal honesty and diligence you demonstrate the high quality of your inward work ethic externally.

Be true to other people in your life. Live in truth with everyone. Never do or say anything that you do not believe to be right and good and honest.

Refuse to compromise your integrity for anything or anyone no matter how great of an opportunity it appears to be. Be gracious and sincere but firm and respectful in declining to accept offers and invitations that will conflict with your purpose.

Always live up to the very highest standard that you know.

THOUGHT QUESTION: **If you ruled the world what kind of world would it to be?**

This question forces you to set high standards for yourself and keep raising the bar. It requires a complete change of heart and mind. You'll discover most people aren't willing to work that

You're The Secret

hard. But they have great respect and admiration for those who are. And will follow an individual with this level of character to success.

Conduct yourself in a way as though every word and action were to become a universal law that could not be taken back once you've spoken it into existence. Carry yourself as though everyone were watching you and pattering his or her behavior after your behavior. And when in doubt, always do the right thing: whatever it is; whatever it costs.

SUCCESS SEED 14

Determine Your Highest Priorities and Focus on Them Single-Mindedly

An attitude to life which seeks fulfillment in the single-minded pursuit of wealth - in short, materialism - does not fit into this world because it contains within itself no limiting principle, while the environment in which it is placed is strictly limited.

-Charles Edwards

Financial wealth is the natural byproduct of personal growth and achievement.

One of the most challenging this to do is train yourself to focus on your highest priorities.

Develop the habit of setting priorities when you're setting goals and objectives. They go together. Concentrate single-mindedly on the ones you want to complete. You will be able to accomplish virtually anything you want in life when you do this. This core strategy has been the primary reason for high income, wealth creation, and financial independence for thousands, even millions of successful people. Sometimes, others will think you don't care. Communicate with them and let them know what is going on before you go into voluntary hibernation. Especially, if you haven't been good in the past in communication this.

On your job, let your co-workers know that you will be closing your door and don't wish to be disturbed. A few years ago I worked for a local college in the area. My program director was good at communicating this. Her method when she came into her office was to say to myself or the secretary very casually, "take all of my calls. I have some very important work to do and will be tied up for the next four hours or the rest of the day".

You're The Secret

She would close her door behind her and that was it. On other occasions she would just come in the office, close the door to her office and we knew exactly what that meant. And we respected it.

Ask your secretary to take messages and not disturb you until your tasks are completed. When you've finished, it's important to cheerfully visit briefly with your colleagues to let them know all is well. My program director would come out of her office check on the secretary briefly and then come down to my office a few steps away and check on me as well or any tasks she'd given me to complete. She was very good at this. It made for an always friendly office environment. Unfortunately there are times when people take offence to a person who's focused on completing a deadline. So be sure to stop and socialize only when you've completed your assigned tasks that you've agreed to be paid for. Remember function like the business is yours and it's up to you to increase your bottom.

When you demonstrate a high level of responsibility with what belongs to someone else it's just a matter of time before you are trusted with what belongs to you.

Your ability to determine your highest priority and then go to work on it to completion is the primary test and measure of your personal will power, self-discipline, and personal character. It is a most difficult habit to develop but the most important one in your life to master if you ever intend to join the ranks of successful people. All human beings love and crave attention whether we want to admit it or not on some level. We all enjoy stimulating conversation however, if we are to attain to the level of wealth we desire, we must develop the essential skills required for completing assignments and tasks.

Below is a list of suggestions for you to consider developing skills in determining your priorities. I trust they will be as effective for you as they are for me.

You're The Secret
Rules for "Thinning Out The Herd To Produce Better Livestock" or "Pruning The Vine To Produce More And Better Quality Fruit."

Everybody can't go with you. As much as it pains me to say this, it's still true. One of the hardest things you'll ever do in life is let someone go. The human body does this quite naturally. The body possesses a built in mechanism for removing those things it knows will eventually cause it irreparable damage. One of those mechanisms is pain. Pain is designed to let your body know that something has happened that isn't normal. It immediately starts to find solutions to alleviate the discomfort. Your body reacts to everything from rushing white blood cells to the injury or going into shock depending on the severity of the pain. Stress, pain and discomfort are the body's way of saying something has to either change or go. Sometimes we allow people to stay around us to long.

My program director Ms. Shawntell McWilliams had a saying, "be careful who you let sit on your front row." Very true indeed.

Successful people understand the importance of thinning out the herd in all relationships and activities. It doesn't have to always be on a permanent basis sometimes it temporary but none the less, it must be done.

List the current activities you're *directly* involved in. These are the activities that demand your mind and body time. These are activities that no one can do but you.

How much of your mind and body time does each activity require from you on a daily, weekly or a monthly basis? Are you expected to be there in order for things to run smoothly? In other words, can everyone get along without you for a season or indefinitely?

Ask yourself; are these activities compatible with each other and with your success goals? Are they inter-related and inter-

You're The Secret

connected or do they always seem to be in conflict with each other in your mind and with your time?

Do they create financial wealth? Do they create a strong sense of inward well being or do they detract from your financial goals?

Can you make a list of the overlaps and conflicts in keeping everything scheduled properly?

Do they meet the five pillars of wealth: Spiritual, Physical, Relational, Educational (Self education and Formal education) and Financial wealth?

Will your decision to thin the herd of some of these projects and activities interrupt or undermine your effectiveness as a person or damage relationships with others?

List the activities you should be focusing on based on how you answered the questions above.

Here is another way to look at the same thing. Use the system that works best for you or use a combination of both when determining your priorities.

Make a list of everything you have to do before you begin working toward any goal. Set priorities on that list by asking yourself these five questions over and over.

What are your highest value activities? What do you do that is more valuable than anything else that adds real value to your work and business?

Why are you on the payroll? What exactly have you been hired to accomplish and are you doing that?

You're The Secret

Ask yourself, what can I and only I do that, if done well, will make a real difference? This is a particular task that only I can do. If I don't do it, it won't get done. But if I do it and do it well, it can make a significant difference in my business or my personal life.

What is the most valuable use of my time right now? There is only one answer to this question at any time. Your ability to determine the single most valuable use of your time and energy is the key that will unlock the vault to higher and more effective productivity and financial success.

Do I really need to add another activity to my life before I complete at least two or three of the tasks that's already looming before me?

Trying to please everybody and adding more things to your life simply because you enjoy them can end up ruining your integrity and give you the reputation of not finishing what you start. Worst yet, it can severely undermine your credibility. It's better for people to say that you're too busy than have them say you're unreliable.

Finally, commit to working single-mindedly on one task, the most important task, the one that creates wealth and staying at it until it is 100 percent complete.

Persevere without diversion or distraction. Push yourself to keep working until the job is done. Remember while you are working, work! This will enable you to break old habits and thought patterns that have held you back in the past. Refrain from bringing more trash for your past.

Everything in you will tell you that you should stop and take a break. After all you've work hard. You deserve a short break and so forth.

Apply the 'one more' rule to help you break old habits. Say to yourself 'let me complete one more page' or 'all I need is one

You're The Secret

more hour; one more minute'. If you're writing or reading a book let your one more be a chapter. If you're writing a song let your one more be another verse before you take a break.

Whatever your 'one more' needs to be for you to complete the task, apply that rule. Soon you will have accomplished what you set out to achieve.

Some people are forced into a place of greatness because of unexpected circumstances that demand they dig deep and discover what they never knew they possessed. Others relentlessly push, force and demand the greatness they know resides within them and then they to rise to the occasion.

Be Great!!! Your choice.

You're The Secret

1. Make a list of your top 20 priorities on your list.

SUCCESS SEED 15

Build On a Reputation for
Speed, Dependability & Punctuality

A good name is more desirable than great riches;

Te be esteemed is better than silver or gold.

Proverbs 22:1

TIME ACCELARATION AND TIME COLLAPSING is the engine of this age and future ages. The one who maintains a supply of having and knowing the right information will fuel that engine and revolutionize industry no matter what that industry may be at the time.

Your ability to download, process, upload and provide exceptional service in real time is your ticket to achievement and eventual success. Everyone today is in a tremendous hurry. Customers who did not even know that they wanted a product or service now want it last week or even last month. Your job as an expert with the right information the first time is to demonstrate to provide expertise in helping your customer know what they want before they know they want it. You must develop the mind set of anticipating what your clients need and have it for them when they need it.

People do not want to wait for anything these days. Loyal customers' will change suppliers overnight if someone else can serve them faster. The reason is everyone has promised something to everyone else based on what they believe can be accomplished within a certain time frame. This is where getting to know your supplier's personally is a priority in your bid to succeed. Your suppliers can make you or break in a matter of minutes now-a-days. The days of waiting until something is aged to perfection are long gone. Instant gratification is no longer fast enough. Your job is to find a balance in all of this insanity and capitalize on it.

Work at developing a reputation for speed, accuracy, quality, dependability and precision. Having the right information at the right time for the right customer will serve you well. Develop a "sense of urgency" as though your life depends on it. Your life may not depend on it but your reputation and bottom line most certainly will. Develop a hunger for action. Be excited about the challenges that will come your way. When everyone else has opted out, you will still be going strong because the things that you've practiced and perfected you are now able to perform.

Move fast always looking for more opportunities. My father in law was a master when it came to finding more opportunities when it came to carpentry work and remodeling. He'd get hired on a job to paint a house and before you knew it he was repairing damaged wood work, repair the next door neighbor's fence and pouring a concrete driveway for another neighbor down the street.

What started out as a one or two day job turned out to be a one or two month job on the same street. We'd always end building a car port or storage shed for someone on that block. Just as soon as the word got around the neighborhood he would be off and running. My father-in-law knew exactly what he was doing and how to do it. He made it a point to always have the necessary tools and equipment in his truck to do a small half of a day job for someone across the street.

Do it on purpose. Do it intentionally. Do it NOW! Develop a system of moving quickly when you see something that needs to be done. Take longer strides while walking when you go to the back of your building. Coming from the back of your building bringing something with you will need later on before the end of the day. Never find yourself coming or going with nothing in your hands.

You're The Secret

Always have something to give your customer or client that will benefit them. Have something they may not know they need on hand to give to them at no additional charge just to say thank you. Just make sure it's something that is genuine, real and has use value. People can detect hype very quickly. Develop a sixth sense when it comes to being able to anticipate what your clients expect and need.

Successful people are known for moving quickly. They have a reputation of attracting and drawing more opportunities and possibilities to themselves and others. So, they get more chances to do more things than those who just do a job when they get around to it. They always stay prepared by having the right tools and equipment on hand.

The saying, 'if you want to get something done give it to a busy person who knows what to do' still holds true. When you develop the ability to drop everything and do a job quickly, your boss or customer will appreciate it. You will be that person who can write their own ticket. Your ability to prioritize tasks plus your commitment to getting them done quickly, efficiently and effectively will move you to the front of the line every time.

Amazing performances will always ensure your seat on the front row of life and you don't have to step on anyone to get there. More doors, than you can ever imagine, will open for you if you are able to develop this skill.

SUCCESS SEED 16

Be Poised and Ready To Move from Opportunity to Opportunity

If I'm Not Winning Then What Am I Doing?
Winning Is All There Is.

-Donald W. Burton

You are geared to win! Every fiber in your being says win. Everything in your nature says winner. I've never met anyone who enjoys loosing and I doubt if you have either. I've never met anyone who gives a victory dance in the end zone because they lost the game. The planet—everything on it and in it—and the universe is ever unfolding and moving toward completion and perfection. You are a part of that grand tradition. Since you're geared to win from birth, you should make preparation to win.

Please understand I'm not talking about winning in manmade competitions and contest. I'm speaking of winning and succeeding at life which is something everyone can do. You were created to win on every level of life.

Life is a process of walking and falling, going forward and backwards, knowing when to hold them and knowing when to fold them, taking two steps forward and three steps back. The beautiful thing about all of this is that every time you fall, you fall forward. Life is designed for you to move forward. People are always walking, driving, and moving forward in motion and in time and space. We do it so naturally that we never stop to think about what is actually taking place and how amazing this dynamic truly is.

You're The Secret

Stop and smell the roses every once in a while. You will be amazed.

Nature is always moving forward never backwards. Everything about nature is progressive. Ever unfolding and showcasing its latest fashions for the season we're in at the time.

When a forest has been burnt to a crisp at first glance that no recognizable life remains. Then the rains return. The charred remains of a once beautiful forest become the fertilizer for the new creation of life hidden below. The dormant seed and root systems of the forest are still there, still intact and untouched by the cataclysmic catastrophe above. Soon micro-organisms, beautiful wild flowers, insects and animals start to appear again as though invited by some unseen painter of canvases and conductor of symphonic masterpieces.

Life, that appeared to have been snuffed out by the flames and intense heat, reemerges bolder than before. This amazing process of regeneration from such destruction demonstrates once again life's resilience to succeed, prosper and transfer life to the next generation. Only the forest's manifestations died but the forest, itself, lives.

Lying beneath the charred remains of disappointments, disbelief, disillusionment, despair, discontent and discouragement in your life are the dormant seeds and root systems that you posses. Ideas waiting to be explored dreams and visions demanding your attention and untold stories of personal triumphs that only you are qualified to tell because they belong to you and you alone. You are created to win, to succeed, and to move your life forward in the most amazing way. Let's get up and dance!

Winning is about coming out of your shell. Even the turtle, in order to survive, has to venture out of its shell at some point. It may not know what awaits it—opportunity or opposition—but there's one thing for certain; if it never comes out, there will be no forward motion for its life. The only time something goes into a shell is when it's hiding, asleep, afraid or dead.

Everything around you is in winning mode. As long as you're moving forward or falling forward, you're winning. All you need do now is learn how to walk for longer periods of time and shorten the times you fall or make mistakes.

Learn from other successful people. Find out what they did in order to start winning. Every one falls and every one walks. The key is to keep moving forward. Winners are always moving forward. Winners are always winning even when it appears they've lost.

Life is made up of cycles; even in business. In business you have cycles, trends, rises and falls. There are ups and downs in all of these. It's built into the system for a reason. Sometimes these processes can lead to a complete change in your industry, your business or your personal life.

We see this today happening in the recording and record industry. Downloading is now the way to buy your favorite music and upload it onto your favorite listening device. This has turned the music industry on its ear and they're frantically doing all they can do to regain their market share.

Life is like the water in a short flexible tube. You can lift one end of the tube and the water will move to the opposite end but the water never goes away or leaves the tube. In other words, for every door that closes another will always—and I mean always open for your next opportunity. You have to be ready to walk through that door of opportunity. Those who are prepared will be the ones to go through that door.

Nothing ever leaves the planet or the universe, it merely transforms into something else. The future of the forest was never at risk. The fire transformed it into something that was even more beautiful than before; something that gave it new life and the new opportunity to sustain itself for hundreds of

You're The Secret

years to come. Devastation is not always devastating sometimes its liberating and demonstrating.

One huge drawback to success is the moving away from the habit of being creative, innovative, imaginative and resourceful. This usually happens when a company moves into the area of maintaining what they've worked so hard and long to create. They start to be mangers of their money. When you do this, you stop paying attention to the things that brought you that level of success in moving forward. Before you know it, you've fallen behind in the very industry that you were once considered an expert in.

Like my college professor once said, 'Behind every successful man there is always another successful man waiting to take his place'. It's the law of transference in its most pristine form. Successful people are aware of this dynamic and because of this, they are constantly on the lookout for a younger person they can mentor and train to take their place thereby allowing the company or business to move forward. Ford Motor Company, Hilton Hotels, Wal-Mart, Sam's Wholesale, just to name a few. All successful people know they only have a certain amount of time afforded to them before they have to begin that transference. Your children, grandchildren, nieces and nephews are great place to begin your transference investment.

Here are a few suggestions that will be beneficial for you to consider and reconsider:

1. Never take your success for granted

2. Always pay attention to the details

3. Make sure that you surround yourself with a diverse demographic of personnel, personalities and like minded individuals and those people who will always find something wrong with everything that's brought to the table. These kinds of people are invaluable when it

comes to critical trouble shooting. People that will challenge your thinking. Iron sharpens iron.

4. Create opportunities to create more opportunities to win.

5. Develop a long-term perspective. Take the long view in everything you do. Project two, three, four, and five years into your future. Visualize already being there and don't allow the short term ups and downs of everyday life to trap you on an emotional roller coaster.

6. Remember, the novel is your life journey and the temporary daily problems, challenges and setbacks are punctuation marks, phrases, grammatical errors and short paragraphs. Keep your focus on the journey. *"And they lived happily ever after. 'The End!* As the late great Paul Harvey, motivational speaker and news commentator would always say, "and now you know...the rest of the story."

7. Remind yourself each day that everything in your life moves in cycles and trends just like the planet and the universe that you are a part of. Stay at peace with yourself, with others and with your surroundings.

8. The more you understand yourself; people and your surrounding the more you will be at peace.

9. Practice being confident, calm and relaxed with short-term temporary pushes and pulls in your wealth.

10. When you have clear goals and plans you are working on every day, the general trend line of your life will be onward, upward and always forward in movement and motion.

11. Every forest that burns to the ground will revive, refresh and regenerate itself into something that's even greater than what it was before.

You're The Secret

1. Do you have any opportunities coming up in the near future that you can take advantage of?

2. Are you ready to move to the next opportunity?

SUCCESS SEED 17

Practice Self Discipline
In All You Do and Speak

*Self discipline is the practiced mental ability to
expect & demand more from yourself and
do more with you than anyone else ever could.*
                                        -Donald W. Burton

Self discipline is the breakfast of Champions. The word discipline in ancient times meant to save one's mind. I would elaborate on that to simply say that it means the ability, desire and determination to save one's mind by paying attention to one's thought, feelings, emotions and conduct.

You can only go as high as your choice of thoughts will allow. You can only achieve to the extent of what you have chosen to meditate on a continuous basis.

Self discipline is a chosen virtue. It is the inward ability to make wise choices when you are faced with remaining on a course that brings failure or taking a path that leads to ultimate success no matter the price you must pay.

It's one of the most important single qualities for real and sustainable success. When you are able to discipline yourself to do what you need to do when you need to do it, you are a self disciplined individual. You no longer need someone to watch over your shoulder because you have crossed the threshold of needing to be externally managed and motivated and have joined the ranks of the self-managed, self motivated individuals.

You're The Secret

When you learn to do a thing and not mind doing it, whether you feel like it or not, your success is virtually guaranteed. You, in essence, awaken and activate the necessary self awareness that helps you obtain the rare prize of self discipline. Success can then be yours to embrace quite easily.

You have demonstrated, by your diligent efforts that you value your inward success and the outward success? It will come to you. The need to strive in the laborious activity of obtaining things is over. You will begin to experience the power of things coming to you very naturally. At this point your success is virtually guaranteed when you are able to master the art of self-discipline.

Success requires a long-term perspective combined with the ability to delay short term gratification. It rests in your ability to set and maintain the long-term goal of becoming financially independent and disciplining your daily expenditures without depriving yourself of certain pleasures that your wealth has afforded you. You must learn to do only those things that will guarantee that you ultimately achieve your long-term goals. Paying yourself first and delaying temporary gratification for long-term rewards is the most simple and fundamental way to move toward self discipline and financial wealth.

Self-discipline can only be achieved by self-mastery, self-control, self-responsibility, self-direction, self-management and self-motivation. Successful people develop the habit of doing things others don't like to do

There are things if life that no one likes to do. Successful people do them anyway because they understand this is the price that must be paid for the success. They looked at the cost of success and set their minds to pay the price through self-discipline and decided that the reward was worth the risk. They know that the rewards that await them are immense and immeasurable so they keep their eyes on the prize before them.

You're The Secret

Successful people are more concerned with pleasing results than pleasing themselves first. Unsuccessful people are more concerned with pleasing methods and pleasing themselves first. If you love pleasure too much you will end up in poverty. I'm referring to those situations in life when you have a choice; not extenuating circumstances like natural disasters and corrupt governments where you don't have options or do you. I've read of people becoming successful in the worst of conditions.

Successful people take actions that are aligned with the goals they want to achieve. Unsuccessful people take actions that are tension relieving and free of pressure.

Successful people do the things that are hard, necessary and important. Unsuccessful people prefer to do things that are fun and easy; that give immediate gratification.

The upside is that every act of self-discipline you engage in strengthens you. It's the law of sowing and reaping at work in all of its beauty. The seeds of self discipline sown today manifest in the fruits of success tomorrow. Every time you practice self-discipline, you like and respect yourself more. you begin to pay attention to yourself on more of a regular basis, what you're thinking, feeling and saying. You start making sure that your words are life giving and inspirational to those whom you speak to. Your dreams, thoughts and beliefs become more important and real than ever before.

The more you practice self discipline in the small things, the more capable you become of the greater disciplines required for great opportunities, experiences, and challenges. You prove to yourself that you can be trusted with more. You cannot get to extra until you first get to even. So be patient with this new process.

In other words if you want to become a world class pianist playing the works of the great composers around the world, you must first learn your concert scales or you will never be taken seriously. You will join the ranks of those who 'already know'

You're The Secret

but have never applied themselves to the action needed to become an expert in their fields.

Everything in life is a test. If you succeed in your time of testing, you then have a testimony. I prefer to call it a 'test of money' which is a fringe benefit of being a problem solver for others. In other words, every test will determine how prepared you are in handling more. The greater the success the greater the tests you will face to maintain your success.

For example, it's about eleven twenty-two on a Monday night and I'm determined to complete the first rough draft of this book. But everything in me is screaming for a coke float right now. The local convenient store is just a stone's throw away and my desire to gratify myself is saying to me, "You need a break. You deserve a break. 'And I really want a break. Talk about being tested in the very thing that I'm writing about. WOW! It would be very easy for me to take a well deserved break and get that coke float and you the reader would never. But, this is what self-discipline is all about. It challenges each of us to ask, do I have the ability to make myself do what I should do, when I should do it whether I feel like it or not?

Only you can answer that.

Dear Reader. FYI *(Today is Friday February 22, 2013. The time is 8:11 p.m. Since I wrote the above statement over three months ago, I've edited and reread this manuscript at least five times and redesigned the cover and the book title about as many. This is my last re-write before I go to print...I think.) Ok. Back to the book.*

So my integrity, as an up and coming bestselling author, compels me to delay my short-term gratification by remaining at my computer and keep hammering this draft out to completion. My "test of money" is in the fact that you are reading this book. There, I feel better already. Hey? I just applied the "one more" principle I talk about in my book.

You're The Secret

Okay, I think you get the picture about self-discipline.

Let me say it again. From the time you wake up in the morning and when you go to sleep at night 'life is a series of tests'. We're sometimes tested even in our dream state. The question is then:

Will you make yourself do the things you said you were going to do? Will you stay with the important tasks until they are completed and will you keep your mind focused on what you need to do and where you are headed?

Thinking and talking about things that are problematic for you only serves to slow your pace and can bring your plans to a screeching halt. Don't dwell on the test. Focus on the testimony instead. Dwell on the steps to making sure you have an astounding 'test-of-money'. You may not be aware of this but some of the greatest achievements and accomplishments in life came from being tested.

Your greatest triumphs will come from your greatest tests. And triumph when tested, translates into opportunities and wealth. Often time's people become experts in their fields from being severely tested. They discovered that their opportunity was disguised as a test. When you're tested you discovered what you're made of and that can only serve to give you a great sense of self respect.

Self discipline demands self respect and the respect of others as well.

Do your coworkers respect you? Do you stay at the water cooler too long? Does a 1 minute break lasts 30 minutes because you feel the need to discuss the company's welfare and its board of directors with your co-worker rather than finishing the task before you go home? Your coworkers may do the same thing but they will excuse themselves and pass judgment on you. To them, their reason is different and justifiable. I can assure you if you habitually abuse company time you're losing valuable influence, my friend.

You're The Secret

Or maybe you're that college student who took a 20 minute trip across town to Star Bucks™ to spend time discussing, with you roommate, 30 reasons why the professor who gave you the homework assignment is such a jerk instead of just doing the homework.

As long as you have excuses one thing is certain, the art of self discipline will continue to evade your life and remain obscure to your vision and the undiscovered country of your mind.

Talent without discipline is like an octopus on roller skates.
There's plenty of movement, but you never know if it's going to be forward, backwards, or sideways."
-H. Jackson Brown, Jr.

Each test you pass moves you onward, upward and forward to the next level of self-disciplined. As long as you keep passing the tests, you keep moving. Self discipline is as light as a feather once you understand it's one of your best allies.

When I first started going to the gym, lifting twenty pounds was excruciating but four weeks later it was no longer a challenge. Challenge yourself to change every day. Get in the habit of evaluating everything you think, feel, dream and say.

Failure can be Albatross around your neck continually weighing you down until you cross the abyss of procrastination into the new country of self discipline.

Remember success begins in your thoughts. If you want to change your life, change your thoughts and actions. The choice is clear.

Your life. Your choice. Your success.

You're The Secret

1. List the top 5 things that you struggle with when it comes to self discipline.

2. Now, list 5 things you intend to do about correcting your struggle.

You're The Secret

SUCCESS SEED 18

Unleash Your Inner Man
and His Unlimited Creative Potential

Potential isn't something you reach but rather acknowledge, develop

and release from within yourself.

-Donald W. Burton

Potential Defined

Potential is...dormant ability...reserved power...untapped strength...unused success...hidden talents...capped capability

All you can be but have not yet become...all you can do but have not yet done...how far you can reach but have not yet reached...what you can accomplish but have not yet accomplished. Potential is unexposed ability and latent power.

Myles Munroe, PhD.

Potential is not what you have done but it's what you have yet to do. It is the ability to dream, think and believe like never before. It's the eruption of creativity that takes place within you when you choose the path of self discipline. You will never exhaust your potential. It is an unlimited creative force of all your genius.

When you have accomplished one thing, you now possess the confidence, courage, precision and resources to accomplish another. It's up to you to unleash this amazing outpouring of personal and ongoing expression. Potential is the ever unfolding possibilities of your creative genius.

You are a <u>potential</u> genius. I underscored the word potential for a reason because genius is nothing more than your ability to download great information through your five senses, process that information with your intellect and power of correct reasoning, discuss it within yourself and with others who will challenge your position thereby deriving at the proper conclusions and then uploading it back into the universe through conversation and healthy communication. That's what genius is.

You are smarter than you believe. You have untapped raw brainpower and creative ability. You just don't know it yet. Most of us, from an early age, had to deal with people and circumstances that consistently tried to and in some cases shut us down. It's like looking for money you accidentally dropped in the trash. You're going to have to dig through a huge smelly dumpster in order to find that bag of trash and retrieve your one hundred dollar bill.

Life is a bit like that. Sometimes you get a lot of garbage dumped on you before you have a chance to discover the real you. So, you grow up thinking that the garbage is the real you because that's all you've ever seen. Then one day you pick up a book like this... Or someone takes the time to say something to you that awakens you. The real authentic you buried at the bottom of that dumpster.

All of a sudden you start enjoying this new and improved version of yourself and the next thing you know you begin to search for ways to stay new and improved. Don't stop until you find...you. That's when life becomes fun and enjoyable. Once you discover those amazing dormant seeds of your true potential you will never be the same again.

Go find your genius. Your Inner Man!

You're The Secret

Your ability to develop ideas to help you succeed is unlimited. This means that your ability to succeed is unlimited as well.

Your energy source for creativity, ingenuity, innovativeness and genius are found in your eight core attributes:

1. Core Passions

2. Core Gifting(S)

3. Core Values

4. Core Interests

5. Core Strategies

6. Core Mind Set

7. Core Beliefs

8. Core Needs

The more you focus your mind on achieving your goals, solving your problems, or answering the thought questions about your business and personal life, the smarter you become. And, the better your mind will work for you in the future.

Your brain, your creativity, is like a muscle. The more you use it, the stronger and more resilient it becomes. You can actually increase your intelligence and your IQ by disciplining yourself to think creatively all day long. And remember, creativity is just another word for *"improvement.* 'Every time you come up with an idea to improve some part of your work, to find newer, better, faster, cheaper, or easier ways to accomplish a result, you are functioning at the highest level of creativity.

Just as you develop your muscles by straining them with physical training, you develop your mental muscles by straining them as well. Here is an exercise for you to develop your brainpower and unlock your inner genius.

You're The Secret

Take a clean sheet of paper and write your most important goal or most pressing problem at the top in the form of a question. For example, you could write, "How can I double my income over the next 24 to 36 months?"

Now, discipline yourself to write at least 20 different answers to your question. Select one of your answers and take action on it immediately. You will be amazed at the results.

SUCCESS SEED 19

Network with Right People

Like any behavior, the more you practice the skills
of networking, the easier it gets.

-Harvey Mackay

Coming together is a beginning; keeping together is progress;

working together is success.

-Henry Ford

Why is long term networking relationships so important? They are like fine wines; they get better with time. You need the right information at the right time to network with the right people. You've seen toddlers; children, young people and adults do this at family reunions, church meetings, athletic competitions and more. Finding common ground and networking is a fundamental human dynamic.

Make no mistake, about 85 percent of your success and happiness in life is going to be determined by the quality of the relationships you develop in your personal and business activities. These are people you know and who know you in a positive way; let me say it again—*in a positive way*. The more you cultivate genuine lasting relationships with other successful people, the faster you will move ahead. No man is an island. If he thinks he is, then he's stranded by himself in the middle of nowhere.

You're The Secret

At every intersection in your life, someone is standing there to either help you or hinder you. Successful people make a habit of building and maintaining a network of high-quality relationships throughout their lives and as a result, they accomplish more than the person who goes home and watches television each night. Let me ask you a very important question. Who do you know if you had a serious financial need and had to borrow enough capital to make a $20,000 payroll you could call at 2 a.m. and they without the least bit of hesitation would come to your rescue?

Strong and lasting relationships are extremely rare and hard to come by and equally hard to maintain over the years. It's probably one of the most difficult things to maintain over time. I think the reason for that is people try to build good relationships based on immediate opportunities and not on common care and concern for the other person, their family and their business.

The unspoken attitude in life is too often based on what can you do for me at this very moment? This type of thinking only encourages mistrust and ill will. Desperation on any level is a thorn in the side of any lasting relationship. Desperate people make poor relationships.

In his book, "Dig Your Well Before You're Thirsty", Harvey Mackay writes about his good friend Zingy. He attended Zingy's sixtieth birthday party and observed Zingy's ability for memorizing the details about people he knew and was amazed at Zingy's vast arsenal of memories. Observing this Mr. Macay makes this observation. And I quote, "these are the results of a lifetime of caring about people, of learning about them, listening to them, spending time, and paying attention. It's the result of a lifetime of networking—that is, a lifetime of asking what you can do for someone else."

It's about finding ways to complete others and not compete with others. Understanding there's enough to go around and if you start to run out of pies just make some more pies. If you do, you will never run out of customers in your chosen business.

You're The Secret

Businesses run out of customers because they run out of innovative ways to serve the ever changing climate of customer satisfaction. They never learn to anticipate where the customer is headed and be waiting for them with the right solution to solve their problem

Virtually all problems in life come as a result of relationships; right or wrong, productive or unproductive. Yet, all of life involves relationships from the microscopic up to universal sizes; between stars, planets, galaxies, the seen and the unseen, the known and the unknown.

All of your great successes in life will be accompanied by great relationships with great people who help you and whom you help in return. This goes beyond the mind set of scratch my back and I'll scratch yours. This has everything to do with true authentic concern for others.

It's important to take advantage of opportunities and not the people who make those opportunities possible.

More than 90 percent of your success will be determined by your reference group. Your reference group is defined as the people with whom you habitually identify and spend time with. How deep can you go in your relationships and networking?

You are like a chameleon in that you take on the attitudes, behaviors, values, and beliefs of the people you associate with most of the time. They take on yours as well. What kind of influences are you passing along to those in your network? If you want to be a successful person, associate with successful people.

Associate with people who are optimistic, happy, have goals and are moving forward with their lives regardless of circumstances. Connect with people who are steadfast in their core beliefs.

At the same time, get away from negative, critical, complaining people or at least limit the amount of time you spend with them.

You're The Secret

Spend 80 percent of your time with the twenty percent of the people who are like minded in their goals. Spend 20 per cent of your time with the 80 percent who are not like minded. Unfortunately, this is a rule and not the mandate because you can't get rid of your family members and people on your job you have to associate with every day.

The only thing you can change in those environments is the way you choose to respond to those who are negative and cynical. You have to take the bitter with the sweet. Remember, you still have the power to choose the way you respond to difficult people. A difficult person is a person that needs additional great information that's all. Your opportunity to be the right example and exert great influence is always possible.

Just remember before you start changing the people you want to be around, make sure you're the kind of person other people want to be around. If you want to fly with eagles you must learn to be an eagle. You can't spend your life scratching around with the chickens. But that's a story for another time.

Successful people network continually. They join their respective industry and trade associations, attend every meeting, and get involved in their groups' activities on the state and local levels. They introduce themselves to people in business and social settings, hand out their business cards, and tell others what they do.

Here is one of the best strategies of all. Whenever you meet new business people, ask them to tell you about their businesses and what you would need to know in order to send clients or customers to them. Then, as soon as possible, see if you can send some business their way.

"Be a go-giver rather that a go-getter." Look for valuable ways to complete your business community. Think of ways to complete and not compete. Always look for ways to put in before you start thinking of ways to take out. Pay it forward.

You're The Secret

The very best way to network and build your relationships is to constantly look for ways to help other people achieve their own goals. The more you give of yourself without expecting something in return, the more rewards will come back to you from the most unexpected sources. You have to keep on casting your bread upon the waters.

Always remember that no matter how smart and capable you are, you can' go it alone.

"If all self made men had it to do over again—they would get help the next time. "

Your life. Your choice. Your success

SUCCESS SEED 20

Take Excellent Care
of Your Physical Health

If man makes it, don't eat it.

-Jack Lalane

Every newspaper, magazine, e-zine or book you read these days, someone is talking about health and exercise. Society has rediscovered the power the ancient and indigenous people knew—if you don't have your health it's going to be difficult to make the other things happen in your life.

In case you haven't noticed, success requires a lot of mental, emotional, spiritual, financial and physical energy. Getting to work before anyone else, staying after everyone else has gone and pushing yourself to new levels of excellence challenges the physical body as well as the mind and spirit. If you intend to achieve the level of success you want, you need to get in the best shape and health of your life.

This is a wonderful time in human history in terms of longevity and physical fitness. Living longer with better quality of life is a reality in today's society. Set a goal to live to be 80 or 100 years better; in excellent health. You can do it. Today, the knowledge and "know how" is available and literally at your finger tips. Take your life out of the hands of the so called experts. Become your own health expert by learning to listen to the language rhythm of your body. It will speak to you.

First, set a goal to live at least 120 years. That's right! I said it, the big 120. Decide that your children, grand children and

You're The Secret

great grand children will not have to visit you in a nursing home facility because you didn't take care of yourself. Sixty has become the new thirty-five. Remember it's all in how you set things up right now. Take inventory of your current health habits and ask yourself whether or not if your current life style will get you to the age of 100 or 120 in great shape.

When my mother turned 80 a few years ago, I asked her how it felt. Without hesitation she said, "It feels wonderful". She also said when she was younger she didn't know if she would every live to be 80. But she decided as a young woman that she would take care of herself so that if she did live to see her 80s, she would be in good health. And, she is.

Mother discovered three simple ways to living a long, happy, healthy and productive life.

The first is proper weight. We need to get our weight under control and remain lean and fit for life. Find out why it's difficult to lose or gain weight. This is important because it isn't always diet. It's not that we're not eating right; it could be that we're not consistently eating right. Think about these four words to starting a weight loss program. "Eat less; exercise more. 'I ascribe to this philosophy for myself. Always leave the table a little bit hungry. Leaving a meal feeling stuffed is unnecessary.

The second is correct food intake. Your body can only respond to the information you give it. It is an amazing and powerful engine but it will only run well on what it was designed to run on; proper nutrition. You don't put diesel fuel in a gasoline engine. It won't work. Neither do you put things in your body that it wasn't purposed to use as fuel.

The key to better nutrition is to eat better foods and fewer of them. Eat more lean meats, with raw fruits and vegetables, grains and healthy drinks. Pay careful attention to food combinations. Do research on food combinations and what your body needs to thrive in today's society. Find out what your blood type is and eat foods beneficial for your blood type. In this day and age of freely available good information, being ignorant of what it takes for your body to perform at peak levels is no excuse.

Eliminate foods containing sugar and wrong fats from your diet. Stop eating white sugar, salt and white flour products. When it comes to nutrition a good rule of thumb is, if it's white it may not be right. Eat smaller portions and eat four or five times a day rather than three large meals. This is a cultural thing. Remember just because it's there, doesn't mean you have to eat it. This is when self discipline comes in. Use your health as another opportunity to exercise yourself discipline.

The third is proper exercise. This requires you engaging in vigorous physical activity approximately 200 minutes per week or an average of 30 minutes per day. You can get all the exercise you need by going for a brisk 30 to 60 minute walk three to five days per week. If you are supercharge about your health, join a health club or get some fitness equipment for your home.

The way to excellent physical health and long life is to set clear, specific goals for your levels of health and fitness. You must make a plan and then follow your plan every day. This commitment to health requires tremendous self mastery, self-control, self-motivation and self-discipline but the payoff will be extraordinary.

Find a personal doctor you can network with and maybe he will end up being your family physician. Get started on a food supplement program and stay with it. Do everything in your power to remain in great health in every facet of your life.

If your financial goal is to achieve a net worth in excess of more than a few million dollars, your health goal should be to live as long as possible so you may enjoy an amazing lifestyle with your money. Your health. Your choice.

You're The Secret

1. Take a few moments to write down your thoughts.

2. Reflect on what you've discovered thus far about yourself.

3. Can you write down 5 things about yourself that you always knew but you weren't sure about.

SUCCESS SEED 21

Be Decisive, Precise
And Action Oriented

The way to develop decisiveness is to start right where you are, with the very next question you face.

-Napoleon Hill

In any moment of decision, the best thing you can do is the right thing.

The worst thing you can do is nothing.

-Theodore Roosevelt

Once again, you need good information at the right time in order to be decisive and action oriented. Bear in mind these skills don't come over night. By diligently applying yourself to what you have learned in these pages and combining that with what you already know, you can't help but succeed.

The things in this book have been gleaned from the minds and experiences of some of life's most amazing people. They've educated themselves with the information they need to make the best decisions possible. They have visualized the results of each action they can take and picked the one with the most probability of success. They think carefully, make decisions and take quick action to carry out those decisions. They are calculated risk takers. They move fast and get quick feedback

You're The Secret

from their actions. *When they find they have made a mistake,* they quickly self-correct and try something else and continue their journey.

According to the Law of Probabilities, if you try many different ways to be successful, you will eventually find that one right way that works for you. It only takes one idea.

According to the Law of Possibilities, there's always at least one more possibility to be considered outside the frame work of normal thinking based on the level of what is known and what will be known.

In other words, Michael Jordan, LeBron James or Kobe Bryant missed a lot more shots that what they've made in their basketball careers but they also made a lot of shots. And the shots they've made have made them legends in their life time. The more they practiced; the more shots they made. But they started with practice—lots of practice. Then they succeeded as great NBA shooters.

After it's all said and done, you have to shoot and shoot and shoot and keep shooting to make winning shots and win championships. Start shooting.

Unsuccessful people are indecisive. They can never make up their minds. They're always hesitant and waiting for *the* perfect moment. So, they don't recognize when that perfect moment comes. Even though they have the right information, at the right time, from the right trusted sources; they don't use it to make sound decisions. They know what they should or shouldn't do but they lack the character, will power and self-discipline needed to make firm decisions. They lack the courage to plunder the vast reserves of creativity in their minds and hearts.

As a result, they drift through life undermining their happiness, fulfillment and success. They never become wealthy or achieve financial freedom. They settle for far less than what they are capable leaving untold treasures of ideas on the table of opportunity for someone else who is prepared, poised and equipped to succeed. They are content to be talkers and never doers. They don't take the time to set themselves up for the very success they long for. Instead they relegate their thoughts to wishful thinking and slip back into a lifestyle of failure and regret leaving the treasure troves of their potential lying dormant inside of themselves.

When you become decisive and action oriented, you shift your entire life into high gear. It's like a jet taking off from the run way. Once the pilot feels those jet engines reach the certain rpm's he'd better be ready to pull the throttle sending the jet liner soaring above the clouds. Like it or not he's committed.

Successful people have developed this sense of knowing exactly when to pull that throttle. They can feel when everything is lined up to make that decision.

Think about all the times in your life when you felt the "magic", when you knew it was the right time to make that decision. Go back and analyze those times. Write down the situation and the circumstances surrounding your decision. What did you discover? What motivated the right decision? The wrong ones?

Keep in mind that when successful people find they have made a mistake, *they quickly self-correct and try something else.* They waste no time in self pity and feelings of failure. Do you?

Success doesn't come by magic or accident. It comes by preparation and preparedness. Remember, victory loves preparation.

When you learn the skill of decision making, you will get far more done in a shorter time frame than other people. This requires preparation. I can't say that enough. Victory loves _____. You should be able to fill in the blank by now.

You're The Secret

I know I'm starting to sound like a broken record but what I say is true so it bears repeating. So, I don't mind sounding repetitious if that's what it takes.

When you understand and apply this principle you actually tap into a higher source of energy, enthusiasm and motivation. Once you get connected you will want to stay connected. This positive energy then propels you even faster toward your intended goals.

A final thought. Make sure that your past successes don't cause you to become complacent in the present environment of your industry or vocation. Just like you came up with a way to gain the edge in your bid for customer service, someone else with a ravenous appetite for success is staying up a little longer than you and getting up earlier than you. They will be on their jobs an hour earlier, stay an hour later and work when they should be working because they're reading this book or some book like this one just like you. Hmm.

The key to triumph is for you to "try" with a tremendous amount of "umph".

Your decision. Your choice.

SUCCESS SEED 22

Failure Is Not Final Nor Is It Your Only Option

Failure is simply the opportunity to begin again,

This time more intelligently

-Henry Ford

Failure is the vehicle that life uses to accelerate your success and progress. Failure has a way, provided you responded correctly of getting you there ahead of everyone else. There is something in every human being and nature that absolutely abhors failure or what we think failure is. You find this to be true on any and every level. Over the years we have learned how to respond to it, handle it, get along with it and even taught our children to do the same. We've even coined clever catch phrases to help us cope with failure like:

> "suck it up and get over it"
> "suck it up, this ain't Disneyland"
> or saying, while clapping enthusiastically, "way to go, that's alright, great effort",
> or my all time favorite, "get over it and move on man".

That's real easy to say when it's not happening to you. I'm sure you heard other phrases and used them yourself in time of crisis and failure. But no matter what you say or do, the lasting sting of failure persists.

Because we have developed the right mechanism to anticipate and handle failure in our minds, we have learned how to live with it.

You're The Secret

At the writing of the final chapters of this book, I found out my daughter failed to pass the bar on her first attempt. When I phoned her this afternoon, I heard the disappointment in her voice when she answered with an extremely weak and defeated, "hey daddy". It was huge. I mean huge. The tone of her voice said everything.

So not really knowing what to say, I said a string of "encouraging" words that was not easing her pain at all. I started rattling off things like, it's going to be ok, there's always another time, I'm so sorry that you failed, your purpose is still intact.

BLAHBLAHBLAHBLAHBLAH! Everything I said sounded so cheesy...*and it was*. After each one of my cheesy efforts she would say a muttered but respectful, "I Know".

Now I'm digging deep because my baby is really hurting and her daddy has to come to his baby's rescue. Right? So what really came to my mind was the most honest and heartfelt words that could ever be uttered from the lips of a human being when they have experienced such bone crushing failure after hours of preparation and study. I said, "what we really want to say is..... DIMM. That's the word DAMN through gritted teeth and clinched jaw. She broke out in laughter stress that you could have cut-with-a-knife instantly dissipated.

After that we were able to have an amazing conversation and discuss her strategy for taking it again. She's scheduled to take the Bar Exam in February. And you know what, she will pass it.

There is something far more dangerous than the fear of failure I've discovered. It's the fear of never trying or never trying again after we've had a bone crushing failure in our lives. Yes, it is true that sometimes you can do everything right and still fail. But, you need to understand that failure is never final. It does not disqualify you from the race nor determine the final verdict or outcome of what you can and cannot do with your life. You are the only one who can do that.

If we started life refusing to try again after we've failed we would have never learned to walk, go potty, feed or dress ourselves. No matter how many times we fell, we got up again. No matter how many times we got food everywhere, we learned to feed ourselves. No matter how often we missed the commode, we finally hit it. All the times we put our clothes on wrong, we kept trying until we got it right. If we hadn't learned those basic skills through the law of transference, we would still be crawling around naked, not able to feed ourselves and needing someone to clean us up and that would be a pretty ugly sight with me being as old as I am.

But we are not that way. And we are not that way by choice and the dogged refusal to quit because we learned from the failures of growing up that is always a "one more time" in each of us.

So, when did we become so afraid of moving forward in our lives?

Fear is a learned response and very pervasive in humanity. It is not fear that we afraid of but it is the fear in something or someone that we are afraid of. Think about it. The bully on the play ground when we were kids that we were once afraid of we're not afraid of any longer. Certain insects and animals that we were once afraid, not any more. The list goes on and on like this. In the course of life, situations and people create enough difficult ups and downs that we know what failure feels like and we learn to fear it.

The thing we have to overcome is the fear that we will look like total failures to other people and be embarrassed when we fail. It is not fear itself that torments us but the fear in something that under minds our progress. Like fearing and anticipating failure.

You're The Secret

That fear must be identified, recognized and conquered. We do that by educating ourselves to the things we fear and the steps we need to take to conquer those fears in those things.

The high school football team was afraid of their cross town rivals until they beat them thirty to zero. Then they were no longer afraid. Preparation, self education and determination over comes fear.

The right response to failure will make you stronger, more resilient and more determined. It is the *fear* of failing that paralyzes your thoughts and activities. It imprisons you in a psychological time warp so that you won't even try to do the things you need to do to be incredible success.

I borrowed the following story but I believe it bears repeating.

A young journalist once asked Thomas J. Watson Sr., the founder of IBM, how he could be successful faster. Watson replied, "If you want to be successful faster, you must double your rate of failure. Success lies on the far side of failure.'

I like that last sentence. Success lies on the far side of failure. It's like I said before, failure is a time accelerator. Before Thomas Edison had a workable light bulb, he had failed over a thousand times in trying to get one to work.

A child walks and falls many times in their attempts to walk without help. Each time they will cry, get up and try once more. But the toothless smile on that child's face is priceless when they discover their God given innate ability to walk on their own.

Successful people are not gamblers; they are masters in the art of taking calculated risks. They are willing to take those risks time and again provided those risks will move them in the direction of achieving their goals; both short and long term. They know they will reap greater rewards for their courage if they don't give up.

You're The Secret

After tremendous failure. Will you dare to move your life forward once more?

Whenever you are faced with a risky situation, ask yourself this question. What is the worst possible thing that could happen if I go ahead?

Do everything in your power to make sure the worst doesn't happen. Get the right information from the right people the first time. But don't let the fear of that worst scenario keep you from moving forward.

That's what successful people do.

Everyone is afraid of failure. Everyone is afraid of lack, loss and poverty.

Quite frankly, we should be. We should condition ourselves to hate all three of them. So much so, that we are willing to be successful enough to eliminate them from our lives and the lives of others. Lack, loss and poverty begin in our thoughts and manifest in our surroundings. The fear of failing will challenge you to make the necessary preparations to not fail.

Successful people are always looking for ways to eliminate these three from the planet. They consciously and deliberately face their fears and take action anyway.

"Make a habit throughout your life of doing the things you fear. Pushing the envelope if you will. The way to overcome fear is do the thing that you fear. If you do the thing you fear, the death of fear is certain."

-Ralph Waldo Emerson

When you act boldly, unseen forces will come to your aid to make sure you accomplish what you set out to do. Every act of

You're The Secret

courage increases your courage and capacity for courage in the future. If you've killed the lion and the bear, then you can kill the giant as well. If you can run a million dollar company then you can run a twenty-five million dollar one and so forth and so on.

Whenever you take action in a forward direction with no guarantees of success, your fears diminish and your courage and self-confidence increase. You eventually reach a point where you can face any fear and have the wisdom to overcome it.

Here are a few of my anecdotes for conquering fear and failure.

To see what it really is, get fear out of your mind and on paper.

Embrace your failures by making them your friends.

Allow failure to be your instructor and guide to lead and prepare you for your next level of success.

Anticipate failure and disappointments ahead of time in order be prepared should they come.

Rehearse various scenarios in your mind and ask yourself how you should respond if these events actually occurred. Determine now to never allow failure and disappointment to disrupt your eight cores.

Be on the lookout for opportunities disguised as failures. Penicillin, a wonder drug of our times, was a failed experiment until some success minded scientist decided to take a closer look at what appeared to be a failure.

Always take a second look before you write something off as a failure in your mind and make the mistake to not investigate it further.

You're The Secret

Find something to be grateful for in every situation in life everyday of your life.

"Failure is not an option; it's an opportunity, embrace it!"

Your responsibility is to commit yourself to becoming a successful person. Focus on that and nothing else. Your job is to set specific goals for yourself, write them down, write them down, and write them down again. Start working toward them every day. You must continue to remind yourself, in the face of all the problems and difficulties you experience, that failure is not final nor is it your only option. Keep looking; there are always gold mines right behind what looks like a failure.

This requires you to re-align, re-focus and re-commit your attitude to one of success alone. That decision, more than anything else, will guarantee you long-term successes.

Your choice. Your life.

You're The Secret

SUCCESS SEED 23

Pass the Persistence Test:
Persistence Is Wisdom

*"Patience, persistence and preparation
makes an unbeatable combination for success"*
-Napoleon Hill

*"Did you hear about the rose that grew from a crack in the
concrete? Proving nature's laws wrong, it learned to walk
without having feet. Funny, it seems to by keeping it's dreams;
it learned to breathe fresh air. Long live the rose that grew
from concrete when no one else even cared."*
— Tupac Shakur, *The Rose That Grew from Concrete*

Persistence is the drop of water that erodes limestone. It's the
ability to stay the course no matter what. Persistence is the
dream behind the mind that wills the heart to believe the
impossible guiding the hands that holds the hammer that drives
the nail that builds the mansion.
Persistence, it's the iron ore and the very core quality of your
character. Persistence reigns supreme. It has no equal.

Persistence is to the character of man as carbon is to steel as
water is to ice. It is the absolutely indispensable quality that
goes hand in hand with all great abounding success.

Here is one of the great secrets of persistence and success:
Program your subconscious mind for persistence well in
advance of the setbacks and disappointments that you are going
to have in your movement toward success.

You're The Secret

Fix a steady gaze on accomplishing your dreams as they manifest into reality.

Resolve in advance that you will never, never give up, give in or give out no matter what happens. Keep finding ways to advance your dreams and goals.

Several years ago a friend of mine told me a story about a dog chasing a rabbit. As the first dog chased the rabbit, a pack dogs saw him running so they began to run with him. As the pack of dogs ran, they soon began to tire. Finally becoming tired, they stopped running because they never saw the rabbit the first dog was chasing.

Be prepared to accept the fact that there will be times you will be the only one who is able to see where you are going. And be ready to chase your vision alone because very few people will ever clearly see what you see.

When you find someone who sees what you see, the way you see and why you see. They are a gift.

When you are overwhelmed with a problem or difficulty, it simply means that you do not have enough time to develop the necessary persistence to deal with the setback or disappointment. Nor, do you have enough of the right information to help you see your way clearly.

True visionaries in their fields always see far beyond the time frame in which they are living.

You're The Secret

Leonardo DeVinci saw submarines, parachutes, machine guns, advances in the medical profession and so much more. But, we had to wait for technology to catch up with what *he* saw hundreds of year later.

Plan in advance for the inevitable ups and downs of living. When they come, you will psychologically, spiritually and physically be supercharged to meet the challenge.

Victory loves preparation. Prepared for victory.

Your greatest personal asset will be your willingness to persevere longer than anyone else. Endure more than anyone else and outlast everybody else. The race isn't given to the swift or the strong but the one who endures to the end.

Your persistence is a true and accurate measurement of your eight core attributes and belief in yourself, your abilities, your understanding of the universe, your need to succeed and why.

All of life is a test. In order to have great success, you must pass the "Persistence test."

Tests can and will come at anytime in your life. They are usually unexpected, totally out of left field or from a direction you would have never thought possible.

You're The Secret

You must realize forward motion will always run you directly in the path of opposition. Opposition is the direct result of your efforts to succeed.

When the railroad was being built to connect the country together, obstacles didn't mysteriously crop up. They were already in the path of the railroad and were encountered as a direct result of forward movement.

Obstacles are opportunities in disguise. Obstacles create the platform for new innovation, imagination and new technology. Never attempt anything while the old suffices your appetite.

Take the persistence test whenever you are confronted with an unexpected difficulty, disappointment, setback, failure or crisis in life. What is the first response in your mind? In other words, what is the first thing you think of? This is where you show yourself, and everyone around you, what you are truly made of. This is where you discover the real self.

Epictetus, a Greek philosopher, once wrote, "Circumstances do not make the man. They merely reveal him to himself."

It is in this place of extreme pressure and stress that you are introduced to the true you. When this happens, there will be nowhere to run and nowhere to hide.

The one inevitability in your life is recurring crisis. It will always be there to greet you whether you like it or not. And if you are living a busy life, you will have some degree of crisis at least

You're The Secret

every two or three months. Along with these crisis will be an ongoing barrage of problems and difficulties for you to solve.

The more goals that you attempt to reach, the bigger your dreams, and the more determined you are to become a successful person, the more problems and crises you will experience.

The only factor you can control is how you choose to respond to difficulties and setbacks.

The good news is that every time you respond in a positive and constructive manner, your strength increases and you become even more capable of dealing with the next problem or crisis that comes your way. Run toward the Goliath's. Do not retreat from them.

Over time you will reach a point in life where you become absolutely unstoppable. You develop a flow about yourself that these things no longer move you away from your goals. You become a force of nature that is even more attractive and irresistible to success and opportunities.

You become the kind of person you once only dreamed of being; the kind of person who never quits, no matter what the difficulty. Regardless of the obstacle in your path, you will find a way to go over it, under it, around it, through it or vaporize it.

You will become more than a conqueror.

You're The Secret

After coming this far in your journey, refuse to be left behind.

Failure can never be an option.

So get up from the mat, there is a fight to win. It's round two.

Your Choice. Your Life.

Live It.

Win It.

Conquer It.

You're The Secret

On A Final Note

The only true constant in your life is you. You can't leave yourself behind. All though if you're like most of us, you wish you could. You're with yourself 24 hours of everyday, 7 days a week and 365 days of the year.

Set your heart to understand what it is you want and need to do to achieve it.

Purpose in your heart what you need to do then do it!

The acquisition of money is only one of many ways that measures earthly success.

Real financial wealth is not in how much money you are able to earn but in how much money you are able to keep.

Your actions can be no wiser than your thoughts. Nor will they ever rise above your thoughts.

Proper preparation is the key to your success. It's in the way you set it up.

Success is in the setup.

Your thinking will be no wiser than your understanding and your understanding will be no greater than the information that you acquire.

The cure for overdrawn and low bank accounts is insight that will aid you in the acquiring of money and to keep money. Learn to make your surpluses earn more money.

The obtaining of wealth requires an entire mental shift and overhaul in the way you think. You must see the need to change before you will change.

You're The Secret

Change is always a choice. It may be forced upon you by circumstance or voluntary made by your own volition but it is still a choice.

True wealth requires a complete and thorough overhaul of you mindset.

You can't take every body with you because everybody doesn't want to go.

You can't get to the land of extra until you get to the land of even.

You're The Secret

About the Author

DONALD W. BURTON is a professional speaker, trainer & life coach, recording artist, musician, praise and worship leader, minister and chairman of GoldMynd Media Group International a multi-media company based company in Longview, Texas. Donald is not a self-made millionaire as of yet but he's well on his way to becoming one.

Donald learned his lessons the hard way. "While being extremely talented I haven't always been very smart", by his own admission. He has discovered that what his father said to him many years ago is still true today. "Use your mind and not just your back."

Donald has never been afraid to tackle any kind of job opportunity. He's been a dish washer and janitor while in high school, worked for the federal government while still in college, been a carpenter, rock mason, a plasterer, a remodeler, painter, salesman, floor and tile contractor, cabinet maker, recording artist, owned his own recording studio, song writer, now writer and author and who knows what else in the future. He will tell you this. He's enjoyed every minute of everything he's ever tried.

Donald is a firm believer in self education and personal empowerment through acquiring a strong knowledge base from personal reading and gaining valuable insight through his own and the experiences of others.

He attended McCurry College in Abilene, Texas where he sharpened his vocal performance skills and stage presence. He was fortunate to be a featured soloist in the touring choir while in college both in the states and Europe. There he received his Bachelor of Science Degree in All Level Music Education.

You're The Secret

Over the years he has been a church musician, director and praise and worship leader. He has started several churches and continues to work with startup churches as well as established churches working with pastors, church musicians and members alike. Donald has a passion to see churches grow and succeed in the Kingdom of God.

He believes knowing the true YOU and tapping into your unlimited reserve of potential will bring about needed changes in every individual thereby fostering a stronger sense of unity among men.

Donald has logged in thousands of hours listening and speaking with people from every walk of life in one on one session and small and large groups. He has taken many of the principles in his book and helped other people go from a life of depression and guilt to one of freedom and success.

Donald is an avid reader and listener of instructional and training books and videos. He believes the key to time collapsing and time acceleration is knowledge and the effective implementation of that knowledge. The fastest way to great knowledge is learning from the achievements of great people. He enjoys reading the books of authors and writers from the industrial period, the Great Book and writers over the past 500 years. He feels strongly that the application of sound information is the fast track to financial growth, personal growth and continued quantifiable development.

His reading library is filled with books on the history of ancient civilizations, their cultures, what caused them to rise and fall and their customs. He loves making comparisons between the old and modern civilizations.

He keeps a library of audio CDs from different authors and speakers and writers in his car at all times. His collection of LP and 78 phonograph recordings, his cassette tapes and CDs reveal that he is very eclectic as a reader and connoisseur of a myriad of musical genres.

You're The Secret

Donald continues to add to his knowledge base in real time as he seeks out new sources such as magazines, old and new books, radio, news, newspapers and more.

Donald loves to acquire and process good information based on his personal experience, and that of others, and combines them into new and fresh experiences every day.

Donald is married, has one daughter and four grand children. He owns a conference & event center in Longview, TX where he lives. One of his main goals is to become an internationally known and recognized motivational speaker.

Donald's personal motto is "Live Your Life One Thought At A Time."

You're The Secret
THE ONE SEED

8/21/2012
by Anthony Othuke Ominiabohs-Nigeria

I do not bask in the delusion
That life is a bed of roses
Neither should the few
Who wish to own a garden of roses

Nature teaches wealth
In little lessons
Lessons man's myopic sight
Fails to see, but the hunger

Do you know, that for your every drop
Of sweat that dampens the earth
You unknowingly sow a seed
That will one day become a tree?

A tree blessed with leaves and fruits
A thousand fruits to quench your hunger and thirst
And more you could sell for a little fee?
A thousand leaves that will shade you from the sun

And more you could squeeze
To aid the sick
A thousand sticks to serve as firewood
And more you could use to mend the roof
Just from one seed that had become a tree?

Do the math and count the trees
If for every day that passes by
A drop of your sweat dampens the earth
And you unknowing sow a seed

How many trees would you own in twenty years?

You're The Secret

How many fruits and leaves would blossom forth?
And if you are to feed on these
From whence will come hunger or disease

If you are to sell twenty thousand fruits
If you are to heal with twenty thousand leaves for a fee
For every season that passes by?
Pray tell what your net worth would be

In the grasses, the plants, the trees
Nature teaches the power of the seed
One seed today can make you a tree
A thousand seeds will make you shade trees

Seeding could be through a gesture
An investment of time and effort
One tree if left to time could make a forest
One seed, good or bad would yield a million trees

And good or bad, so shall the reward be
In deed and gesture, evil seeds will multiply like weevils
In a bean farm, so keep your sweat pure at all times
For every seed will bounce back a thousand times

If you wish to own a garden of roses
All you need is sow a seed, nurture one or more trees
Patiently watch it grow and amid seasons watch it row
A bed of roses into your tomorrow

Made in the USA
Charleston, SC
24 October 2015